Ladies From Hell

SERGEANT R. DOUGLAS PINKERTON

Ladies From Hell

With the London–Scottish Regiment
During the First World War

R. Douglas Pinkerton

LEONAUR

Ladies From Hell
With the London-Scottish Regiment During the First World War
by R. Douglas Pinkerton

First published under the title
Ladies From Hell

Leonaur is an imprint of Oakpast Ltd

Copyright in this form © 2011 Oakpast Ltd

ISBN: 978-0-85706-689-3 (hardcover)
ISBN: 978-0-85706-690-9 (softcover)

http://www.leonaur.com

Contents

To
The Girl
Who
Waited
My Mother

Foreword

I realize the utter futility of writing a preface, for no one ever reads one—unless by chance they be in a hospital or waiting in a dentist's office. It is for these unfortunate few, then, that I indict the following.

After you have been through the mill and mire of battle, your life is changed. It can never be the same again. It seems that you must still continue to fight, even though you be physically incapacitated.

Therefore it is partially for my own amusement, and partially to continue my fight for ultimate victory that I write this book.

In it I have endeavoured, in a meagre way, to tell America what she wants to know. You are asking about the same questions as did England in 1914 and 1915. You are in approximately the same position as was England in those early days. You are beginning to discover that business cannot be as usual, and that war is not all flag waving and hurrahing. You are learning, as did we; and may a just God grant that your lesson be shorter by far than was ours.

My efforts will be devoted to a truthful presentation of what I saw and what I know. There is little humour in warfare. That little I will try to preserve. My endeavour will be to loan you my eyes for a space that you may see what I saw, and thus know your war—for it is yours—just a wee bit better.

I hope, as you turn the last page, that you will realize the true meaning of this struggle, that you will realize why I take pride in having been a member of the London Scottish, and that, above all else, you will realize the true duty of your America today.

In closing let me express my appreciation to C. H. Handerson for his assistance in arranging the multitudinous incidents of my fighting days in some sort of sequence, and in helping me to weave them into a connected story of my little excursion with *The Ladies from Hell*.

(Signed)   R. D. Pinkerton.

Copy of Telegram to Colonel Malcolm from Field Marshal Sir John French, Commander-in-Chief of British Forces.

I wish you and your splendid Regiment to accept my warmest congratulations and thanks for the fine work you did yesterday at Messines. You have given a glorious lead and example to all Territorial Troops who are going to fight in France.

Copy of Letter to Colonel Malcolm from Major-General E. H. Allenby, G. O. C. Cavalry Corps.

Dear Colonel,

I congratulate you on the accompanying message from the Commander-in-Chief, which you and your grand Regiment have so richly deserved. I wish to add my sincere thanks, and those of the Cavalry Corps, for the self-sacrificing support you gave in a great emergency. The behaviour of officers and men of the London Scottish was worthy of the best traditions of British Regular Troops. Only their steadiness and courage saved a situation that was as difficult and critical to deal with as will ever occur.

> Yours sincerely and gratefully,
> (Signed)   E. H. Allenby,
> Major-General.

Copy of Letter to Colonel Malcolm from Brigadier-General C. E. Bingham, Commanding 4th Cavalry Brigade.

My dear Colonel,

I venture to ask you to convey to your Regiment my deepest gratitude and admiration for the work they performed on October 31st, and through the following night. No troops in the world could have carried out their orders better, and while deploring the losses you have incurred, I unhesitatingly affirm that the Allied Armies in France owe to the London Scottish a place of high honour amongst their heroes.

> (Signed)   C. E. Bingham,
> Br.-Gen., 4 Cav. Bde.

Nov. 1, 1914.

CHAPTER 1

How the Call Came

From a hospital cot in Flanders the story came, from the tongue of a jawless, nameless man. I and a thousand like me read it, and read it again; then, along with the other thousand, I went down to the drill-hall to scrawl my name on the list of Great Britain's soldiers.

It seemed awfully odd to be there, for only three months before I'd teetered on the curb, not a block away, and seen our boys of the London Scottish marching off for their baptism at the front. They'd swung along very spruce in kilt and khaki, and in the haze of August 4 the war seemed a long way off.

As they passed, their pipers struck up that old favourite of mine, "The Cock of the North," and I wished rather vaguely then that I might have been along with them. The crowd cheered in a hearty, happy way, and I envied our boys, and I intended to join them—sometime. But I delayed, because, like the rest of us, I was asleep on August 4.

Even the boys in khaki underestimated the task before them. They had marched away before, they'd been cheered and wished Godspeed before, and as old Johnny Nixon passed me he called out, "Hello, Pink, old boy, I'll see you again at Christmas"; and I and the rest believed it. But that was August 4.

So they marched away, gay and hilarious, almost out for a summer stroll, and only Lord Kitchener knew or suspected the trial that was to come; and he kept silent.

Today it was November 1, and of the thousand who had marched away only three months before, a scant three hundred remained. Johnny Nixon had gone down with the rest.

Joffre's Frenchmen had swayed the German line back thirty miles, from Paris to the banks of the Marne, and trench warfare had begun. Slowly we folks back home began to stop joking about three-year enlistments as an impossible term; the casualty lists were longer, and England was waking up. And then came the story of Hallowe'en night. The Scottish, our Scottish, whom we seen go not three months before, had been in action. They'd mobilized just outside of Paris; been rushed up in the pink of evening, in motor-lorries and afoot, to stop the onrushing Germans.

Far off to their right they heard firing; like breakers on the shore it sounded, dull, tireless, meaningless. And then, as they drew nearer and nearer, the sounds took on distinctive meaning. Individual shell-bursts separated themselves from the vast jumble of noise, and then were lost in the ceaseless roar to the rear.

It was half-past eight when they got there, and night was just coming down. They halted and stood at ease, while their colonel climbed up on a broken cart and addressed them. Then, with his good wishes and Godspeed, they stumbled off to their trenches, mere threads on the face of the earth.

On their left were the Lancers, on the right the Carabiniers, both regular regiments. Our Scottish were just volunteers—volunteers with orders to hold their ground.

The night wore on till ten o'clock. Off in the distance they heard the Germans coming, flushed with their victories. They made no attempt to hide their approach, and "*Die Wacht am Rhein*" floated down to our men in the trenches.

On they came; one could almost see them now, but the British had orders to withhold their fire until two hundred yards, and they held it. Wave on wave the German troops came on, and wave on wave they were mowed down; but there is an end to physical endurance, and in time numbers will tell. The regular troops to the right and left fell back, and left the Scottish, our Scottish, alone, with the cream of the Prussian Guard at their front, on their right, and on their left. Perhaps if our boys had known their predicament this page would never have been written; but, being just volunteers, they had only their orders to go by, and they fought on and on.

There were only a thousand of them, and three times they formed up their thinning ranks. On their third attempt the Prussians broke and fled, and our boys returned to their lines, leaving some five hundred and fifty behind in the mud and mire of old Flanders.

But that isn't all the story. Back with them came a stranger, a German officer. A bit of a scratch on the head had knocked him out for a time, and our stretcher-bearers carried him in, along with our own wounded and dead.

In those days (we have learned more since) we knew nothing of German *Kultur*. In those innocent, early days a wounded man was a wounded man, no matter what his creed or his colour or his race. So our boys took the German and treated him as one of their own, and turned him over to old Doc McNab for attention.

It was only a wee bit of a scratch he had; but Doc leaned over him first, while our own wounded and dying lay waiting, and as he finished his work the officer asked for a drink from his bottle, which he had thrown down on the floor.

Gad, we were innocent then! They'd not even bothered to remove the Hun's service revolver, which dangled from a strap at his side; and, as old Doc McNab leaned over, the German's right arm twitched, there was a flash, and a tiny thud. The Teuton sprang to his feet, his revolver still grasped in his hand, but old Doc McNab lay still where he'd fallen.

That was the story that came from the hospital cot in Flanders. It was enough for me. I awoke. And when I got to the drill-hall there was no mistaking the place, for from a block away you could see the crowd. A long, thin line of young fellows wound in and out of that crowd, each in the grip of that story of the night before. I took my place at the end of the line and waited.

Hours passed.

In the meantime the line strung itself far out into the street, for from all over the country men had come swarming in. Tall, lanky Scots they were mostly, from up northward, crystallized into a solid fighting mass by the story of the Marne and the tale of the London Scottish.

In that line there was little talk, though the crowd hummed like a hive. We volunteers were silent. Here and there perhaps was a burst of laughter, but it was rare. Most of us were thinking, and thinking hard. As the hours crept slowly by and I shifted from one tired foot to the other, the enthusiasm which had filled me at the start began slowly to ooze out and away.

"Was it worth it?" I questioned. "Belgium outraged, treaties broken, friends gone, and I was going; but was it worth it, after all?"

And other men were debating, too. Dark scowls of self analysis clouded many a face in that line, but not a man stepped out; for the glorious example of the London Scottish, the thoughts of our friends, and the empty cheer that "perhaps we wouldn't see action, anyway," combined to hold us in line.

I might as well be frank. Four hours of waiting on a chill November day is likely to take the romance out of even war itself. But there was enough of romance there, just enough and no more, to hold me in that line from four until eight that night.

At eight came my turn to be examined. A brusk and worn officer, dark and pouched under the eyes, peered up at me in an impersonal sort of way from under his vizor. He took down such minor details as my name and address, and directed me to step into an anteroom, where I stripped, and then I was ushered into another room with two or three other chaps.

Here we were hurriedly examined for physical defects, and a flush of primeval pride crept over me as they fled from my ears to my eyes and from my eyes to my feet without finding anything the matter. Long and tediously they lingered over my feet and knees and leg muscles. The wait became painful, so thorough was their work about these apparently unimportant parts of my anatomy; but at last I was officially marked as O. K. and fit for service.

Little attention had been paid to my peculiar fitness, by either education or experience, for any particular branch of the service. These tired and hurried men in khaki seemed much more interested in how soon I could report for active duty than in aught else concerning me. There was nothing about my examination that would lead the casual observer to think that Great Britain had spent time or forethought in selecting from this mob of men those specially skilled in this or that branch of industry. We were men, all of us, just men, and Great Britain wanted men, and in those dark days of 1914 many a man who could have served his country better at the bench or in the workshop was rushed trenchward and lost, with all his potential usefulness.

Hastily I dressed and joined the silent group of some fifty or sixty other chaps who waited in an anteroom to the right. There we stood, staring morbidly at one another. There was nothing to be said; comradeship was banished by the solemnity of the moment. Occasionally a time-worn joke would be passed among the groups, and the laughter was just a trifle forced and hollow. Some of us made brave attempts to hide our thoughts—thoughts of home and mother, family, and all that. What little talk there was was rough, inclined to *braggadocio*, punctuated by laughter that rang peculiarly out of place, like laughter in a doctor's office or in a morgue.

14

Abruptly the door opened, and we were herded into a darkened room. At a table sat an officer in uniform rumpling through a mass of blue and yellow papers. Before him stood an inkwell and a Bible. A hooded light cast weird shadows over us, and we stood about, first on one foot, then on the other, and waited. For a time he worked feverishly, meanwhile grunting out hoarse, unintelligible orders to a pale and anaemic-looking chap who dashed in and out of the room like some automaton.

Suddenly—so suddenly that most of us jumped—he stood up, and swung the Bible over his head with the habitual movement of a man practising his morning exercise.

"Raise your right hands and repeat after me," said he. A forest of hands shot up, and we repeated, word for word, the solemn oath of allegiance of the British Army.

"I hereby swear by Almighty God that I will bear faithful and true allegiance to His Majesty King George V, his heirs and successors, and will obey as in duty bound commands of all officers set over me, so help me God."

"Now kiss the Book," said he, and we kissed that dog-eared volume with various degrees of explosiveness and enthusiasm.

I was now a soldier of the British Empire. I had been duly accepted and sworn, and, truthfully, I was rather disappointed at the feeling. I looked no different, I felt no different, unless it was for a sense of duty done and suspense ended. I was rather dazed, but at a pointed hint from the recruiting officer I picked up my hat and departed for the quartermaster's stores. It was now ten o'clock at night, and the order was to appear the next morning at nine.

The details of our preliminary training in London would be of little interest to the average reader. It varied little from that now being given your boys at their respective camps.

The short days of November and December flew by quickly enough, with marching and counter-marching, bayonet-fighting, and light field work, all intensely interesting at the time, but soon forgotten in the new duties and new excitements that were thrust upon us.

Gradually our flabby civilian muscles took on a more sturdy texture. The kinks crept out of our desk-bent backs, and our sallow civilian skins became bronzed with a rosy admixture of sheer health, while the seventy-five-pound service kit ceased to be a herculean burden of leaden weight.

As we marched and fought our mimic wars, grim reports drifted back to us from the firing-line in France, sometimes mere haunting rumours, sometimes the sullen facts themselves; and our faces grew grimmer, our practice less mechanical and more intense. Something of the spirit that had dominated the London Scottish on Hallowe'en came to us, and all sense of dread, conscious or unconscious, vanished. But the gulf between us and civilian London grew ever wider. We were nothing to them but a passing show, interesting, perhaps, as an incarnation of the fighting spirit of England, with a certain charm as examples of the impetuosity of youth, nothing more. England slept, though the war was already in the fifth month of horrible reality. The people of the London streets, the happy, carefree, busy throngs, drifted on in a mist of unreality, while we lived, and lived intensely. Not that they could fairly be blamed, however. It was not their fault that they looked so resolutely the other way while Louvain and Rheims and Ypres were shattered and burned. We soldiers received news, some of it authentic, some sheer rumour. But no such news ever reached "the man in the street." He was an outsider.

The newspapers were hammering out ream on ream concerning the brutality toward Belgium. Dark hints occasionally burst forth, flickered on the popular tongue, and died. An uncompromising, uneducated censorship kept the real facts darkly closeted, and though the newspapers knew much, their inky lips were shut, and the masses devoured miles of newsless news, while the facts crawled from lip to lip, and only empty rumour told the truth. When some fact, red from the firing-line, actually did slip from under the clumsy thumb of our early censorship, enlistments doubled and trebled and quadrupled instantly. A Zeppelin raid, fortunately, could not be stowed away in a musty cubbyhole, and hence did yeoman's service for our recruiting officers. But while the civilian, fed on vague nothings for the most part, dreamed on peacefully, we soldiers in the making, who received the real news from returning veterans, blazed in earnest fury to be done with our training, and over and at the enemy in fact.

Late in December came orders to inoculate us for typhoid, and we rejoiced, for we knew that our days in London were now numbered. When the medical chaps appeared, we lined up dutifully and laughingly watched their advance. No more villainous-looking array of venomous little needles had I ever seen before.

Now, a typhoid inoculation is a simple thing. Like marriage, one never appreciates it at its true value until later. As fast as we were treated, we were given forty-eight hours' leave of absence, "on our

16

own," surely a silly precaution for such a tiny pin-prick! But the omnipresent brain of headquarters seldom errs in its directions, nor did it err this time, for I was scarcely half-way home when I was seized with a sudden and unaccountable clammy coldness that traversed my spine in elephantine shudders. I chattered into the house, a picture of frozen misery. All afternoon I hugged the roaring fire in an agony of chills, all night I shook and chattered gloomily to myself upon a bed piled high with blankets. Not till the wee small hours of morning did I cease to curse the idle jests that I had flung at the toy weapon of that grinning medical officer.

Then came notice that we would start for our intensive and final training at Dorking, on January 1. With this news came the Christmas holidays, and some of us who were among the fortunate romped homeward, bursting with health.

Not even all the spoiling I got at home, however, during those few days, and the real pang I felt at leaving, could dull my enthusiasm when I went back to join my regiment, bound for Dorking, the first step toward France.

Dorking is, or rather was before our arrival, a little town of some five thousand inhabitants; but by December its population had doubled, and soldiery swarmed its streets by day and night. The town faded into the background like a frightened child, and the inevitable kilt brightened an otherwise colourless winter landscape.

From six-thirty in the morning until five-thirty at night, and often until the gray of coming dawn, we drilled and drilled and played at fighting. Thousands of straw Teutons were annihilated daily. Our rifles, at first clumsy clubs in our hands, gradually became a part and parcel of us and of our daily lives; and happily so, for when you are ploughing through the mud of no-man's land the only friend you have is your rifle. No single piece of training stood me in better stead than the incessant training at handling our Lee-Enfields.

Our rifle-practice might destroy some of the cherished delusions of the armchair theorists. The ranges were usually from two hundred to six hundred yards. It is within that zone that the rifle-bullet does its sweetest work, and at two hundred yards, when a wild mob of howling Huns are belching down upon you, or you on them, the dainty rifle-sight is well-nigh forgotten. Its coy outlines are those of a stranger dimly seen and hardly recognized. You slap your rifle to your shoulder; no time for fancy beads and adjustments of wind-gage. It is just a case of shoot, shoot hard and fast, and may a kind Providence and a skilful doctor look after the poor man who fritters away his precious seconds in pretty logarithms.

At the front, unless you're sniping, the rifle-sight well-nigh loses its identity. Fine, hair-splitting arguments about it are forgotten, and sheer instinct, guided by the rifle-barrel's blackened bulk, is enough, as the notches that might decorate any Tommy's gun would indicate.

Don't misunderstand me. The rifle is no apprentice tool. It is not used to hammer nails or tacks. With all his apparent nonchalance and carelessness, your Tommy or your *poilu* (Fritz, too, I dare say) regards his rifle as his most cherished pet. He puts in hours a week upon its pretty mechanism, oiling, polishing, truing, always and everywhere; for the canny Tommy knows from cruel experience that the day may come when between him and the grim reaper with a German name stands only the shadow of his rifle.

Winter settled down, and with its shortened days the pace became faster, the training harder, always harder. Regular hours'? We had none. It was just train, train, train, from field to rifle- range, from rifle-range to field again. Play it was, hard play, but news from across the channel spurred us on, and we yearned to be over helping, and avenging our brothers who had gone before.

But the end was nearer than we knew.

At 4:30 one morning (it was ghastly cold, with three or four inches of mica-like snow swirling underfoot and rasping into the bare flesh) we were routed out of our bunks to entrain for Epsom Downs. Like lightning the word ran down the line: we were to be reviewed by the Iron Man of the British Army, Lord Kitchener himself.

By 5:30 we were on our way, and in a short half-hour we tumbled out of our refrigerated coaches into the most blinding snow-storm of the year. Through it we trudged, each an animated snow-man, and then from six until eight-thirty that morning we awaited the arrival of the great Lord K. of K.

But it was worth the wait. A splendid figure he was, big upstanding, a man's man from his boots, black against the snow, to the vizor of his immaculate cap, impervious alike to man's petty criticisms and God's storms.

Chattering with cold, we marched by in stiff review, and then lined up before him and listened as his big voice boomed out above us, brief, terse, to the point, a message worth the hearing.

"Men of the London Scottish, you have a record to uphold. Three things only would I leave with you today, you soldiers of the British

Empire. First, fear God; second, honour your king; and third, respect the women." His voice caught, and he repeated with added emphasis, "Respect the women."

Then, with a brief nod of dismissal, he thanked and congratulated our colonel for the splendid appearance of his men, and disappeared into the blinding snows.

No trains were waiting to bear us back. They had long since gone about other and more important business, and we were left to plough homeward through fifteen miles of sodden sleet and slush.

Then came the call; one hundred and fifty of us were going to France immediately. Some kind fate smiled on me, and I was among the first of our battalion to be selected. There were brief, but hearty, congratulations from the unfortunates who remained behind, and we of the favoured few were off for forty-eight hours' leave before entraining for Southampton.

Forty-eight hours is a niggardly enough allowance for some occasions, but forty-eight hours before departing for the battle-front is an everlasting hell of torment. My first advice to any soldier in similar circumstances is to go to the theatre, the tavern, go to any place but the place you want to go, home. I say this because I know what those last forty-eight hours cost my mother, though she showed the terrific strain but little.

It was a Sunday night; I remember we had been to church together; my mother, my sisters and my little dog, Rags, walked to the station with me. I wished devoutly that they had stayed at home, and yet I valued every minute with them as my life, and blessed the long walk and the belated train.

All about us were other men and other women, some talking excitedly, feverishly trying to cram into a moment the thoughts and hopes and prayers of a lifetime. Others stood silently, crowded close together, seeming to suck some modicum of comfort from their very nearness. Porters—there were porters then—brushed past with professional zeal; trains shrieked and roared; people came and went, bumped us, jostled us, but we felt them not a bit. We and those others about us were living in the past and the future, and all mankind might have roared by and we would not have seen or felt their going.

Even the little children seemed awed by the unaccustomed atmosphere about them. Women with babies in their arms held them up for a last fond caress of a khaki-clad father, not too proud to show a glistening eye. One chap—he sat next to me—was going back for the second time, and he leaned far out of the quaint old English coach to implant a last kiss upon the candy-covered lips of a pink little cherub.

My mother watched and chatted until the final preliminary jerk told us that we were on our way. Then she waved gaily to me, and flung me a last brave kiss. I thought I saw her lips quiver for an instant, but she bent to pick up Rags, who was making frantic efforts to board the train, and when she straightened again her eyes smiled, steady and brave, above his wriggling body.

At London we entrained for Southampton amid the cheering strains of that ancient Scottish dirge, "Will Ye nae Come back again," truly an inspiring note to waft after a bunch of trench-bound soldiers. At Southampton we were given the allegorical keys to the city and more freedom than was good for some of us. The group to which I attached myself made a valiant, but wholly vain, endeavour to consume the entire stock of some score or more ale-houses, and the results were not unusual.

I must admit that I have only faint recollections of a rather rough and toilsome journey to the camp-grounds. There was a moment of awful concentration as I endeavoured to gather my scattered wits sufficiently to pass muster as a soldier, sober and sedate. Then came an agony of fear as I realized that I had failed in my endeavour; but a kindly provost marshal shut his experienced eye, and looked the other way, and the only punishment that awaited me was the usual morning of repentant thirst, and an awful fear of the effects of the channel-crossing upon my addled pate and stomach.

At dusk, the following evening, we embarked for France, cheered on by half of Southampton.

The dock was as black as the Styx itself, but the ship was even blacker. There were the usual false starts and cries of late arrivals, the usual turmoil and bustle, and then, as the chimes struck out eight o'clock, the dock noises suddenly became dimmer, as if a multitude of gauze-like curtains had been let down between us and them.

We were off. At the Southampton bar two powerful search-lights cut through the night and pinned us to the darkness. Through their rays flashed a torpedo-boat destroyer, a dashing black shadow smothered in spray. Semaphores wigwagged up and down; a searchlight wavered drunkenly. The tiny destroyer dashed to starboard and encircled us, round and round, like some joy-crazed fox-terrier pup. Our engines increased their steady thumping, and we were off—off for France!

THE LONDON SCOTTISH ENTRAINING FOR THE TRENCHES

CHAPTER 2

France

Choppy Channel seas, proverbial the world over, a reeling world underfoot, scudding clouds, bully beef, hardtack, and a night of well-earned, but unwisely spent, revelry, mixed with the same gladsome cordiality that distinguishes oil and water. From eight that evening until midnight, I decorated an unsteady, but extremely popular, rail. But who shall say that even the darkest cloud has not its silver lining? Had it not been for that ill-timed mixture of tempest and toddy, midnight would not have brought with it a sight that will cling to me until my last reveille dies away.

We were four hours out, fighting through solid sheets of salty spray, when away off to the east a dim glow welled up from the horizon. By indistinguishable degrees it grew into a ball of yellow light, and a hospital ship rushed out from the mist, homeward bound, with its pathetic cargo.

White as bleached linen she was, with a huge red cross of mercy painted on her side and illuminated to all the neighbouring seas by a powerful searchlight hung from her rail. Brilliantly lighted at her foremast-head was a tremendous Red Cross flag, held out stiff and taut by the nipping breeze. At the stern a Union Jack floated, and about her rail a band of alternate white and green lights set this ship apart, beyond all mistaking, as a vessel that held nothing that she feared to show.

As far as you can see her a hospital ship is a hospital ship and nothing else. Out of the night, like a torch, she springs, and into the night she speeds, bound for Blighty, for home. Such ships it is, these white messengers of mercy, plainly marked, that the Hun sinks "by inadvertence." She passed, and we held on our course through the thick blackness of the night.

Out of the morning mist came France, and down to the boat to meet us pushed a great sombre-coloured throng, of women mostly. There were a few men, old fellows, and a scattering of chattering little children.

Colour! There was none; it was black everywhere. Even in those early days France was a mourning nation. The Marne had cost. Mons had cost. They are four years past, and still, even today, France fights on.

The France of the *boulevardes* and *cafés* is not and never has been the real France, any more than the children of your comic supplements are the real children of America. The real France is a nation of impenetrable depth and strength, grim and everlasting.

As we skipped off from the boat, the cheery faces of a few American women called to us. Before them were great piles of rolls that tasted like home, and huge urns of steaming coffee belched forth untold gallons of renewed life to wave-worn Tommies.

You can have no realization of how delicious a roll and a steaming cup of coffee can be until behind you is a night on the English Channel, and before you France and the fighting-line.

Up into the railroad yards we moved, after a brief rest, and then war—the first intimation of it—jumped out at us. Gone were the English coaches, with their unappreciated comforts. Before us was a string of very ordinary and very dingy box-cars, boldly labelled:

Hommes 40
Chevaux 20

The above, which was translated by the more worldly-wise among us, referred to the ability of said cars to carry forty men or twenty horses. Personally, I am convinced that someone made a grievous error in figuring the carrying capacity of these cars. I was one of the forty "*hommes*" in one of them, and the proverbial sardine must feel lonely in comparison to us. Twelve hours of jolting added nothing to our joy, although it served to shake us into a more perfect fit within the car. Never will I complain of the five o'clock rush on your street-cars. With all its horrors, it is a stroll in the park, compared with a twelve-hour massage in an antiquated perambulator, labelled by some practical joker, "*Hommes* 40, *Chevaux* 20."

Rouen, our destination, was a funny, squat little town, amusing in the extreme to us of London's busy thoroughfares. We whistled our way along its funny little cobbled streets just as church was letting out, for it was Sunday. Lined up on each side of us were rows of chattering French folk, three deep. Apparently the war was forgotten for the moment, and we in our kilts became the chief topic of discussion. Gay jests were thrown out at us, and were returned in kind, but the Frenchmen had the best of it. I remember one little gamin, with the shrill yelp of the street urchin, nearly wrecked the regiment by loudly calling attention in surprisingly good English to the marvellous shapeliness of our captain's legs.

The enjoyment, however, was not all on the side of the populace. We of the London Scottish, many of us bred among the rattle of trams and the roar of trains, found plenty that was novel in the curious old town. Its fifteenth century architecture, its thatched roofs, its jagged skyline, and whitewashed walls reminded one strangely of the second act in one of Raymond Hitchcock 's comic operas. I almost expected to see the inevitable brewer from Milwaukee rush in, escorted by two wax-moustached *gendarmes* and followed by a weeping soubrette and a crowd of irate villagers. There were plenty of soubrettes and villagers; we lacked only the German brewer. He, and a hundred thousand like him, were forty miles away.

Our camp, or base, was at the top of a hill over- looking the town. Long avenues, cobbled with unthinkably cobbly cobble-stones and lined with funereal-looking poplars, stretched away before us. Neat little houses, each with its flaming garden, broke up the wayside into homey patches of colour. Over it all swam the dust from our pounding feet.

At the base we were given a riotous welcome by the older soldiers, some of whom had already gone, to return slightly wounded, while others had yet to see the whitish, cotton-like plume of exploding shrapnel.

Friendships were struck up immediately; word from England was exchanged at par for word from the fighting-line. In time, facts gave way to rumour, rumour to gossip, and at last gossip itself resigned to the unceasing chaffing and friendly "strafing" that is a sign of healthy, happy camp-life.

The days were largely our own, and the motion-picture theatre and the canteen, with its delicacies, did a land-office business. Fifteen thousand of us boys were there. What little routine we had was similar to that of the training-camp back home, but there was a slight difference. The orders were sharper, the officers looked more tired and careworn. Everywhere there was an atmosphere of tension and strain, a waiting for the call that would start us flying trenchward.

And one night, at 9:30, that call came. I and a dozen or so of my new-found pals were attending a moving-picture show. I remember that Charlie Chaplin had just completed some target practice with a large and succulent cream pie when the alarm rang out. We dashed out into the night without ceremony. At the alarm-post was our officer. The Germans were breaking through our lines. We were to be off immediately. We stumbled away through the dark to get our packs; and then the bugle sounded again, and it was announced that we would move early in the morning.

It was a real relief to know that after five or six months of training we were to be released from the leash and freed to do our bit. Like prize-fighters were we, in the pink of condition, eager for the gong and the test. Our bodies were rested, our spirits superabundant. Fear? There was none. There was no room for fear in the excitement of the moment, for tomorrow we were to become, in deadly earnest, members of Great Britain's fighting forces, and we longed for sun-up, as a schoolboy longs for Christmas morning.

Sun-up finally came, red, then yellow, and a glorious morning unrolled from the east as we marched away to the railroad station and the train that was to take us to the front.

The scenery was no longer a novelty, but, in our intoxication, peculiar modes of dress, and odd colloquialisms gained a renewed amusement for us, and were again held up to rude banter and ridicule. But the French laughed with us at our jokes or at our French; for they had come to know Tommy, and they knew that his bark was a hundred times worse than his bite.

The British Tommy, you know, is not a bad man at heart. He loves to chaff and chatter, and the French have come to love him, with all his faults, almost as well as they love their own *poilus*. There is something so solid and stolid about the British Tommy that it appeals by contrast to the Frenchman, used as he is to his volatile, excitable countrymen. It is the Tommy's stability, his solidity, that makes him valuable, especially when mixed with, and cooperating with, less-experienced troops. He steadies the line, gives steel-like tenacity to its backbone, and grim, unquenchable determination to its morale. But to see your British Tommy cavorting on the green of a rest billet or about a railway depot, you would never suspect him of those sterling qualities for which he is justly famous.

While we waited for the train bedlam was let loose. French people were *burlesqued*, French trains were imitated, everything French came in for its share of ridicule, and the Frenchmen stood about us and grinned and enjoyed it with us. They knew better than did we that despite it all we loved France, and would love her still more as we gave more to her great cause.

All day we waited for that train. Thanks to the Y. M. C. A., hot coffee and rolls were forthcoming, and, be it known, at a shamefully small sum. We of the wise, who had held council with veterans of similar uncertain trips, filled our haversacks with chocolate, hard-boiled eggs, and bread, as fortification against possible vicissitudes of wartime travel, and we did well.

Ultimately the dilatory train, such as it was, pulled in, amid jeers and cheers from the assembled soldiery. It was a decidedly dilapidated-looking little train, made up of ancient third-class coaches, loose-jointed box-cars, and first-class coaches, remodelled to suit the momentary need.

Like a Sundayschool class out for a picnic we piled in. After an interminable argument, all were seated, and the officers repaired to the platform until a fitting moment of departure should be granted us by a crabbed looking train-despatcher. No sooner were the officers out of the door than a full third of the car left by the windows on the far side, to return, triumphantly bearing luxuriously upholstered seats from some empty and neighbouring first-class coaches.

I suspect that future Baedekers will earnestly beseech American tourists to bring their own cushions when travelling in France, for I am quite sure that another year of war will totally denude French first-class coaches of such luxury.

Evening drew on, and it was with difficulty that the rickety coaches bore up under the strain within; but, perhaps because he realized the impending danger to his train, the despatcher finally let us loose, and we were off for the front, just as night closed down upon us.

Immediately the blinds must be drawn, for Teuton airmen have been known to spot such speeding trains and to bestow a bomb or two upon them, or perhaps a dose of machine-gun fire cast in at open windows. But we were not in total darkness; no such luck. Above us, thrust through holes in the roof, were consumptive oil-lamps that served rather to emphasize the gloom than to dispel it. Nevertheless, these aspiring, but inadequate, lamps were at premium, and one enterprising Tommy, at the risk of his own life, crawled along the roof of the rocking train and pilfered the light from our compartment that he might the better mend a slight tear in his equipment.

But gradually the practical joking ceased for lack of further food to feed upon; conversation dwindled, and one by one we dropped off into the land of nod, surrounded by the fumes of the dilapidated oil-lamps and by a few wakeful souls whose voices droned away tirelessly throughout the night, telling and retelling little anecdotes of home life, of London, and speaking of their hopes and fears for the future.

The night wore on amid the rattle and groans of the train, and those half-indistinguishable noises of the dark as it slipped by us. But with the first faint rays of morning came another sound entirely new to us; and yet it was not a sound at all at first, but a feeling of omen, a sensation of vibrations too low in degree to shake our tiny ear-drums. Gradually it became more and more pronounced, and all at once, as if a door had been opened, the clean, clear bark of an English field-piece burst in upon us, punctuated by the sharp crack and crash of German high-explosive shells.

Instantly the train was a hive of excitement. *Bark, bark, boom* came back those waves of sound. A window flew up, another followed, and the full and incessant roar of distant battle surged in with the morning sun.

War!

It was in the air, and yet it was nowhere.

Little peasant houses, stage-like through the mist, sent up wee columns of smoke from their kindling fires. An old man, dressed like a page from a nursery-book, puttered in his garden, but straightened up and waved to us as we fled by. A tiny little town popped past, another, and then another, and the inhabitants toddled to their gates and waved and called in the high *falsetto* voices of old age. An automobile, with the chauffeur bent low over the wheel, plunged round a corner and stopped in a cloud of dust and explosive French expletives; and through it all and by it all we raced, while the tumult of battle became ever more audible.

After an unforgivably long time the train stopped, hesitated, and crept into a station. On the platform were a group of kilted officers, representatives of the battalion to which we were going. Stiff and sleepy from hours of travel, we lumbered out of the coach, amid a clutter of equipment, and lined up, while the waiting captain briefly and hurriedly welcomed us to our new quarters.

Then, with two pipers at our head, we swung eagerly out into a cross-road, turned to the left, and stretched out, a long, party-coloured line, down one of those typical, cobbled French roads, lined with its long, lean poplar-trees.

A staff automobile, drab-coloured and mud- spattered, flashed by, oblivious of ruts and bumps and all other traffic. At a cross-road a seemingly endless line of huge khaki-coloured transports, laden with food and ammunition for the front, rumbled and rattled by. All day long this line wound on, endless, tireless, a monument to the tremendous appetite of war and to the efficiency of the British War Office.

By the wayside quaint little thatched peasant huts crept up to meet us, and crawled away into the dusty distance. Old folks—always old folks—toddled about, pursuing the humble duty of their age to the grim accompaniment of distant, but continuous, gun-fire.

At last we trudged into the town of Alougne, where we were billeted. I, fortunately, was quartered with an old French woman, a wrinkled, bespectacled old grandmother of wondrous sweetness. Her "boys," she called us; "Mother" we called her. There were thirty-five of us stationed with her, and, as I came up, some of the boys who had just returned from the firing-line were noisily enjoying their first bath in five weeks.

We of the new draft looked on wide-eyed, worshiping the naked heroes of the trench, and later some of a more practical turn of mind helped our adopted mother with her little household chores, her garden, or her much-beloved cow. One of the city-bred chaps of London gallantly offered to milk her cow for her.

"*Non,*" said Mother Lecoq, smiling broadly at his blissful ignorance; and then, in exquisitely bad English: "One tried to milk her las' week; he still *dans l'hopital Ma vache* no friend of Tommy." And with that Mother Lecoq rolled off with her milking-pail to do the task herself. After viewing *ma vache*, I am inclined to believe the tale.

By evening the old-timers were sufficiently washed and polished to satisfy even the most fastidious, and we gathered around our coffee and milk, with an appetite whetted for the tales that were certain to come forth with the dusk and the reminiscent glow of lighted pipe and cigarette.

After considerable coaxing, Pete—we never did learn his last name—grudgingly agreed to tell of his latest escapade in no-man's-land.

Pete was about as big as a minute and as bashful as a two-year-old child. To extract a tale from him was a task; but, once in it, he gave himself over to the telling with a gusto of a professional raconteur.

It seems that he had been given orders to take a little excursion out into no-man's-land in order to locate a German machine-gun emplacement which had been proving needlessly annoying to one of our communication trenches for two or three days.

During the day he took his bearings and arranged a private code of signals with the listening- post from which he would depart, and to which he planned to return after the completion of his task.

Promptly at the appointed hour he went over the top and stumbled across the pitted surface of no-man's-land. Everything went smoothly enough, and he was well on his return journey with the desired information stowed away in his pocket when a flare hissed up into the sky and turned no-man's-land into a river of calcium light.

At that moment, Pete was only about seventy yards from the German trenches and he prostrated himself with a curse and a prayer for luck. As he fell, his eye caught a movement to his left, and he dimly saw three helmeted figures, like himself grovelling in the mud, German reconnoitring patrols in no-man's-land.

Instantly he ripped his revolver out, but returned it to its place with equal despatch, for in such circumstances indiscriminate shooting is the height of folly. Any shot in no-man's-land is likely to bring down a hail of bullets from both the opposing trenches—bullets that seek out friend and foe with equal favour and equally disastrous results.

There is an unwritten law, founded on stern necessity, that governs no-man's-land. While all patrols in this forbidden territory carry revolvers, they are seldom used, for obvious reasons. When hostile parties meet, if they be of equal strength, they pass each other with an exchange of horrible threats, but little else. However, if one patrol is stronger than the other, it may endeavour to capture the weaker party, but always without firing, if possible. Firing a shot in this God-forsaken territory is like lighting a match in a powder-magazine. It is about as certain a method of suicide as has yet been discovered.

But to return to Pete. The German patrol was only about twenty or twenty-five yards from Pete when the flare flashed up, and as darkness again settled down they worked so close to him that he could have touched them, had he been in a careless mood. Discretion, however, was Pete's middle name, and he let the Germans lead him by thirty or forty yards until they halted squarely between the outreaching arms of two English listening-posts.

At this psychological moment Pete, in his eagerness, tripped and fell full on his face with a resounding splash. Instantly the three Germans dropped, and Pete resigned himself to what appeared inevitable capture. But for once the inevitable failed to materialize, and the Germans set on about their mission and moved ahead until they were within one hundred and fifty yards of the English trench, and still exactly between the two outstretched listening-posts.

Then Pete took his life in one hand and his revolver in the other, fired into the night in the direction of the Germans—and hopped into a listening-post. The report was not dead on the air before no-man's-land was ablaze with flares, and the three Germans were neatly trapped squarely between the English listening-posts.

The German line, scenting trouble, started up a fusillade, effectively preventing their own comrades from returning homeward in the intervals between the flares of exaggerated daylight.

During a momentary lull in the firing, while the English flares were withheld, a strong reconnoitring party went out from the ends of our listening-posts, which were about seventy-five yards apart, and neatly pocketed the Germans, who were found cursing lustily and worming slowly Berlinward on their stomachs.

Pete's experience provoked similar tales, some of actual experiences and some of a lurid nature that would make *Diamond Dick* and his associates as green as mint with envy.

One story I remember particularly, for at the time it struck me as being ample proof of the necessity for rigid discipline in trenchland.

It seems that an officer, accompanied by six men, planned a bit of gum-shoe work in no-man's-land. Word of their plans was passed down the line, and at the appointed hour they set out. On returning, they had approached to within thirty-five or forty yards of their own trench, when a lance-corporal called "Tiny," because he was six feet five in his stocking-feet, let fire at them with a speed and energy imparted by six months' incessant practice. Tiny had forgotten his orders, and did not recall them until a familiar and acid voice boomed out from before his rifle-sights:

"You damn fool, you! Want to kill your own men!"

Tiny collapsed on the firing-step and hurriedly computed the possible extent of his damage and the probable severity of the forthcoming punishment. More by good fortune than design, however, his aim had been as bad as his intentions had been good, and therefore six weeks at hard fatigue was the punishment for his temporary lapse of memory.

It was amid a hurricane of similar incidents that the evening wore on. The men seldom if ever spoke of casualties, confining themselves rather to the humorous side of trench life or to tales of rare professional skill of one sort or another.

To our avalanche of questions they gave only patronizing, tantalizing answers.

"Oh, you'll soon find out, my boy," was the usual response to some query that had been quivering on our tongue for hours.

"How does it feel to be under fire? Well, were you ever in a bathtub of hot water when—well, you just wait and see. You'll find it's almost exactly as I have been telling you. 'T would be a crime to spoil the feeling for you by describing it too minutely beforehand."

But out of their idle conversation I gathered that of all war's manifold horrors the most dreaded is the waiting under fire—waiting to go over, to do anything that will expend your pent-up energies and nervous force, anything that will stop your thinking, anything that will stop your imagination from running riot and making a coward of you despite yourself. Within a fortnight I sounded a loud "Amen" to these complaints.

During the course of the evening they repeatedly lamented the death of a certain Tommy Thompson, their machine-gun sergeant. Tommy, it seems, had been busily engaged in scattering his steel-jacketed gifts among the Germans with marked and invariable success. But success brings with it its own penalties, and early one morning, prior to their usual eleven o'clock Hymn of Hate, the Germans started throwing over some heavy stuff as a token of unusual spleen. These shells were surprisingly well timed, and appeared to be focusing perilously near to Tommy's machine-gun emplacement. A little to the left they dropped, and then a little to the right; then one to the rear by five yards, and then one a bit to the front, but always creeping closer, like the flow of a horrible tide.

Here the storyteller paused, and spat reflectively at the barn-door before continuing. The others stared hard into the fire.

"I was out at a listening-post," resumed the speaker, "when a shell went over my head with a noise like the "Flying Scotchman" on its run from London to Glasgow. I felt in my bones that she was the one that was going to do the work; and she did. I looked back, and saw the whole emplacement and most of the neighbouring scenery thereabout heave up into the air in a cloud of nasty, brownish smoke. When the wind caught it away, there wasn't anything left of the place, and where old Tommy had been dozing was just a bit deeper than the rest.

"I went back when my time was up, and met one of the machine-gun crew coming back with Tommy's identification disk in his pocket and the remnants of the machine-gun on his shoulder.

"'That,' said he, 'is the sixth one they have clicked for us in the last week, and I'm going back to get another.'"

After this recital there was a prolonged silence. Tommy Thompson had been extremely popular among his mates, and one by one they withdrew into the cow stable, which was our *boudoir* for the nonce.

This particular cow stable, I soon learned, was on a par with its thousand fellows of northern France.

It was alive with rats of an embarrassingly friendly disposition. That was my first experience with rats on such terms of intimacy. To this day a rat running across my face will wake me, but that night a rat scampering across my wrist sufficed to wake the echoes of the entire neighbourhood. I was sternly cautioned to be scrupulously silent, else I might wake not only the echoes, but the remainder of the rats. This sage advice had the desired effect until two of the little creatures engaged in a friendly sparring match, within three feet of my head. I hastily seized my rifle, and managed to place its butt neatly upon the upturned face of a chap three rows farther down the line. Forthwith I was pronounced worse than the Boche himself, and was deposited outside of the shed for the balance of the night, that my comrades might enjoy the silence and the rats undisturbed.

But even in the open I was not alone. At three o'clock I woke with a feeling that was a cross between an itch and a bite. Shortly, however, the itch disappeared completely, and gave way to a series of unmistakable and undeniable bites. The "crawlers" were among us. Crawlers, be it known, is a popular and esthetic cognomen for lice, plain body-lice. They are particularly friendly with the Scottish, owing to the comfortable quarters afforded by the Scottish pleated kilt.

By morning we of the new draft were thoroughly aroused to their presence, and an astonishing and horrible array of germicides appeared in protest. Most of us had come armed to the teeth for these much advertised creatures, and we longed to try conclusions with them.

The conclusions, however, were all in favour of *Monsieur* the Crawler. He is invincible. Powders guaranteed to kill anything on four feet or centipedes, are as nothing to his Satanic Majesty. A patent grease with which you are supposed to butter your body appears to be a haven of refuge and a mine of nourishment for him.

After experimenting for a few hours with all our powders, greases, ointments, and a mixture of all three, we retreated before the inevitable, and joined that day's crawler party about a bonfire, in which our contributions were deposited as fast as we could locate them and convince them of our earnestness.

And over us always floated the tireless boom and crackle of the battle. We wanted to be in it. The older men, with their good-natured bantering, had made us feel woefully out of it. We longed to duplicate their experiences, to be able to speak casually of bombs and shell-fire, as if we lived and thrived upon the stuff. There was no feeling of fear or dread; but the nervous strain of waiting, coupled with the monotonous work about the billet, had its usual effect, and soon, for lack of other amusement, Tommy, new and old alike, fell back upon his genteel and ever-handy pastime of grousing.

This business of grousing is Tommy's foremost and dearest accomplishment. He didn't invent it, but he has perfected it to an unbelievable degree. If Tommy can't grouse and grumble about the weather or the fit of his socks, he will pick upon his sergeant. If the sergeant, by some stroke of Deity, is flawless, the commissary department will be aired to the breezes. If the commissary department has furnished agreeable grub of late, 't will be the post-office which has failed in its duty. Always your Tommy will find something seriously wrong if he really sets out to do so. But at the bottom of it all is nothing but a big heart and a desire for a little encouragement and sympathy; which, if not satisfied immediately, begets the desire to have revenge on the nearest object. Grousing is nothing but a poor substitute for sympathy, and it is as harmless and as meaningless as a lassie's smile.

For four days we rested and ranted in our billet behind the firing-line, while the grumbling of Tommy and the growling of the battle-front became steadily more noticeable. Which of the two rumblings brought the welcome order to be off, I do not know; I only know that it came, and early on the fourth day of our stay we formed up and prepared to leave.

As I ran out of the gate to join my company, our old hostess called to me, and, flushing like a schoolgirl, breathlessly handed me a wee bundle.

"*Voici, mon fils,*" she said, "you keep him, an' do not forget *moi et ma vache.*"

With that she turned back, waved me a pretty goodbye, and threw a kiss to all of us as gaily as a maid of one fourth her age.

I opened her humble packet, and a worn and battered rosary fell out into my palm. Touched by the sentiment, I poured it into my breast pocket, and to this day I carry it, half as a talisman of good fortune, and half as a reminder of old Madame Lecoq and her indomitable *vache*. She calls up a vision of all France personified, that gay old soul who had given her three sons, yet, for all her sorrows, kept a brave spirit.

As we swung away through the village, bent old figures waved to us, some gaily, some gravely, from each little doorway and garden, and a horde of chattering children followed us, just as I used to follow a travelling-show, wide-eyed and wondering. Far out to the edge of the town they trotted beside us, and would have continued on indefinitely, I firmly believe, had not we ourselves ordered them back.

And how we hated to see those kiddies go! French they were, foreign to us as foreign could be, but kiddies still, and reminders of home. To send them back was to snap the last tie that must ever link man to home and fireside.

As the tail of their chattering procession disappeared around a bend, we settled down to the wearisome grind of march. Dust welled up all about us. It was hot, desperately hot for May, and our tongues soon became thick and leather-like. Some of the boys sucked incessantly on malted milk tablets, and what a godsend they were. Aside from their slight nourishment, they helped wonderfully in alleviating thirst, the grim spectre of which dogged us all day long.

By noon we had covered about half our journey to Richbourg St. Vaast, but only a fifteen-minute halt was allowed before we were again up and away, gray, dust-covered ghosts plodding through a mist of chalky atmosphere. Toward evening a sky-line rose up to meet us. It was the high-water mark of the German advance in that sector.

What the name of that village was I do not know. It was lost with the village itself, perhaps. Not a house was left; as far as the eye could reach to the left and to the right was only ruin and then more ruin. A chimney, gaunt and unreal in the evening light, jutted up into the sky; a solid wall, perhaps, or a roof, but never the two together. Through some broken wall or open doorway one could still see the little homey scenes, a bed, a chair or two beside a shattered hearth, a table with the dishes still resting on it. In the centre of the village stood what was once a church, now a rubbish-pile of blasted brick and multi-coloured plaster. In the ditch beside the road were occasional dead horses, loathsome objects. A lean dog rested across the shattered threshold of one house, and nearby, in eternal truce, were the battered remains of his ancient enemy, the family tabby; but the family were gone, unless the little cross in the doorway and the mound of new earth perchance marked the last resting-place of the owner.

Such sights were new to us, and they had their full effect. Laughter and talking died, and curses, mumbled through clenched teeth, took their place. The spirit of France sifted down upon us and took up its abode in our hearts.

From soldiers in name, this village, a habitation fit only for crows and scurrying rats, turned us into soldiers in fact; and as we stumbled wearily on, grumbling was gone, and grim, silent determination had taken its place—determination to avenge those roadside crosses, those homes, and, yes, that lifeless dog and cat, dumb, but eloquent symbols of homes violated, firesides wantonly wrecked, women and children murdered or carried away to a bondage more horrible by far than death itself.

Our billet that night was a war-racked house. The windows were gone, the door swung drunkenly on a broken hinge, the garden was a hole half filled with brackish water, the walls were staggering uncertainly, and the little orchard was a mass of charred and jagged stumps. It had been a home once, and a home it was again to a score of dusty, kilted Tommies; for Tommy's home is where he hangs his hat.

But scant time we had to enjoy its rude comforts, for ten of us were ordered out to the firing-line. Our excitement was intense; but it was dampened when, instead of guns, we were handed shovels, and, instead of cartridges, pickaxes. War, you know, is not all shooting; ninety *per cent*, of it is hard, laborious work.

After being cautioned to make no noise and to beware of all light, we stole forward through the night to a point about four hundred yards behind the firing-line, where a communication trench required lengthening and deepening. Here for the first time I saw the scene for which I had been in training these six months past.

Spread out before me like a panorama, as far as the eye could reach, were the trenches, outlined by hundreds of twinkling, flashing star-shells, some red, some green, others yellow or white. Blot out the sounds and the unmistakable odour, and it might have been a fireworks display at some summer amusement-park. But the sounds! Who can describe the sounds of no-man's-land and its environs at night? There is the nasty hollow *rat-a-tat-tat* of the machine-gun, now far off and dull, now sharp and *staccato*, like a snare-drum, as its hungry mouth sweeps in your direction. Then comes a series of echoes, hollow, sinister echoes, that you feel as much as hear. A spent bullet whistles past you, and dies away in the distance; a big gun booms down from afar; and over it all rises the intangible sound of men moving, living things living, or transports groaning up, and a medley of nameless noises that arise from nowhere, yet are everywhere in no-man's-land. And all about you is the smell of dank water, of blackness that is all the blacker for the distant star-shells, of dead and living things, all bound together into an odour that is the property of no place but no-man's-land.

As we began to dig, the heavens opened up, and in five minutes we were ankle-deep in mud and blaspheming our way through the stickiest soil that ever cursed mankind. It took superhuman effort to get it on your shovel and equally super-human effort to get it off. The Creator made that soil to stay put. As we struggled with our shovels and picks, a merry company of rifle-bullets, directed at no place in particular, kept up a medley of falsetto whines above our heads. Off to our left had been a wood,—I use the past tense advisedly—for now there remained only a collection of stumps and prostrate branches outlined black and phantom-like against the sky. To our right was an ancient cabbage-field long since gone to the great beyond. Hour on hour we struggled on through that gum-like soil, until my knees wobbled and my breath came hard; but I, like the others, laboured on.

There is something about the firing-line that tightens your sinews and lends a triple toughness to your muscles. I have seen men fight for days, uncomplaining and unfatigued; I have seen them fight for days and labour for nights without thought of rest. I have seen men go through the trials of hell, and do it smilingly and easily, apparently blessed with an unfailing fountain of strength; and then I have seen these same tireless workers go back to the billet when their labours are at an end, and collapse in a heap, spent utterly.

There is a species of auto-intoxication that pervades trenchdom. Men are dying all about you, and in the face of death, life's uttermost efforts seem puny and small. Of course you never really reason it out that way, at least I know I never did; but the fact that others are sticking it out, that others are holding and giving their all, must have an unconscious reaction that draws upon unsuspected wells of nervous and physical strength.

Perhaps no such strength buoyed us up that night. It was probably the excitement and the novelty of it all, for it is a novelty to hear bullets whining past when the swiftest messenger of death with which you have had experience is a London taxicab; it is a novelty to picture the Huns crouching over there, a few hundred yards away from you; it is a novelty that I wish every man might experience, and stop with the experiencing.

Just as the first hint of morning specked the sky we stumbled back to our billet, tired as no human was ever tired before. Not a man spoke; even the firing-line was passably quiet. You could hear the German transports pounding along faintly over the cobbled roads, and I remember vaguely wondering why we didn't drop a shell in their direction. A "greenhorn" is likely to be remarkably generous with ammunition.

No hot meal awaited us, just a scant pile of straw that looked better and felt softer than the mattress in the guest-room at home. Four hours flashed away, and the morning broke with the comfortable sound of a British field-piece barking away angrily, like a little dog at a treed cat. I tested myself experimentally for symptoms of a cold, but found not the slightest trace.

It is an interesting thing that despite the horrible and all pervading dampness of the firing-line there is little sickness. In the midst of all the hardships and privations there seems to be no room for the petty annoyances of civilian life. It is seldom that a man visits a medical officer. Blistered feet are the soldier's foremost ailment, yet many a man will go for days with his feet blood-soaked from blisters rather than seek a medical officer for remedies. It is not bravado; in the trenches you don't place much importance on such things. After all, life is a matter of comparisons. You are rich in my estimation because I am poorer than you, and I am comfortable despite blistered feet, because you have lost an arm or perhaps a leg. So it goes. In the midst of death there is no room for colds or fevers. There are so many more expeditious methods of making your exit from this world that the old-fashioned maladies have quite lost caste on the firing-line.

Our next billet was another empty shell of a house, afloat on a sea of mud. All the land thereabout had seen much of shell-fire, and presented the general appearance of a huge black lake that had been beaten into a raging fury and then frozen as it ran. Huge holes, great billows of earth, with brambles and bricks floating in weird, unnatural positions upon its surface.

For several days we worked at odd, meaningless jobs about the place, gathering a vast fund of information and experience. I presume that this is what we were supposed to do, to become acclimated to the sights and sounds, to familiarize ourselves with the *modus operandi* of the front-line. We rapidly became rather set in our ways. Like old bachelors, we acquired little idiosyncrasies. Experiences that would have filled a volume a month before were now ignored and forgotten; and why not? Here we were, hovering about the brink of the Hun-made hell. We never expected to return to familiar sights and sounds except on crutches or on a stretcher; so why should we become ruffled at the sound of an onrushing shell? Fatalism? Oh, perhaps, but not bravado; just a stoical complacency that takes possession of you after the first five or six shells have failed to make you their mark.

I don't mean to say that shell-fire is welcome. No man who speaks the truth can aver that he has any hankering after the heavy stuff. He may become accustomed to rifle-fire, to the red-hot hell of machine-gun fire, but shell-fire has a horror all its own. You never really get accustomed to it, and it is for that reason that many men are captured after a heavy shelling. They are unhurt, but the horror of continued shelling saps their will to fight, and leaves them dumb and dazed and void of all will to think or do.

It was in this atmosphere of stray shells and rifle-fire that we acquired our trench legs. Then came the order to move up another notch. This proved to be six hundred yards from the front trenches, and for the next three days we had box-seats for the grand performance. From the real we approached what was once the unreal, and now the unreal proved far more real and much more full of life than the most important event of our little yesterdays.

My first night at the new billet I was detailed off to ration fatigue, which in plain English is the job of getting the company's rations from the cook. Our cooks were stationed at a spot known as "Windy Corners," so named because of the Teuton's earnest endeavours to wipe it out of existence.

The Teuton, let me say, is a wise bird, and he has an uncanny way of knowing your movements before you yourself become aware of them. French civilian traitors are usually to blame. In fact, nothing so endeared Sir Douglas Haig to the men as his order relegating non-combatants to the rear by fifteen miles. After this order went into effect the Hun's remarkable guesswork fell off markedly. Prior to that time I had seen instance after instance where traitorous guidance was evident.

One peculiarly clever case comes to my mind. Near us, at one time, on the firing-line, was a house. For days we called it the "charmed *château*" because it alone of all its neighbours remained standing. In

The sergeant's Cook's Instruction Class

our early innocence we marvelled at it, and talked vacantly of supernatural causes, until an officer remarked a rather striking coincidence. When any considerable company of our men went forward through one or more communication trenches, the chimney of the "charmed *château*" would emit a sudden series of smoke-puffs, and instanter the German shells would begin to flit about with remarkable exactness. In the telling it seems simple enough, and yet no one had noticed this coincidence before.

There was an elderly woman living in the place, and I can testify that she was a marvellous cook. Her home, partly by reason of her kindness and her cooking, aided, perhaps, by her remarkable immunity from shell-fire, soon became a gathering-place for our officers. She was always most solicitous about our health, and showed an apparently justifiable interest in our movements. She also had a dog. Even the dog was friendly, and, like the woman, was soon adopted as a part of our trench family. But for the canniness of one of our superior officers she and her dog might still be dishing out soup with one hand and shrapnel with the other.

When suspicion was at last centred upon her, the first move was to watch the house and the dog. Two days later the dog appeared innocently meandering homeward from the direction of the trenches. Three Tommies waylaid the unaccountably shy Fido and abstracted a neat bundle of German memoranda from his tubular collar. Our dear French friend had kept the Hun batteries well supplied with full data, and the mystery of their remarkably well-ordered fire disappeared forthwith.

Two hours after her arrest her home was visited by a German high-explosive shell. Who told them of her arrest? Ask the Huns. They have a system all their own.

But to return to "Windy Corners" and the cookers. The roadway ran parallel with the trenches and within tempting rifle-range; but it was nearly eight o'clock and dark, so that Bill Nichols and I scampered along with little fear of detection. We reached the cookers, we filled our sacks, and we started back, quite overflowing with the joy of living and a great contempt for our enemies across the ditch.

There was a fool with us. I was that fool. I started whistling "Tipperary." About the first eight notes had been confided to the night air when a bullet hit the road three feet in front of me, and *pi-i-i—nged* away in the dark. I needed no second invitation, but dropped "Tipperary," the biscuits, and everything that would impede my rapid progress, in a heap on the road, and made a run for it.

The billet was all there to meet me, including the sergeant.

"Where are the rations, Pink?" said he.

"Down the road, sir," I replied between puffs.

"What the hell? Down the road?" he countered.

I explained that machine-gun fire had no great allurements for me, and that therefore I had departed rather hastily without the rations. But my sad tale produced no sympathy, only an order to go back and get the grub.

My progress on the return trip was *via* a ditch, which put twelve feet of solid roadway between me and the Huns' rifle practice. Half-way back I met Nichols, progressing stealthily like a child with a stolen cooky. He, too, had discovered the ditch and was making good use of it.

My return with the biscuits was the reverse of what I had pictured. I had visions of being welcomed as a hero of some note, perhaps of being mentioned for bravery under fire; but I was acidly informed that ten days' extra fatigue was my punishment for not obeying orders. I had been told to bring back the rations, and I had returned without them.

For the benefit of the reader I will pass over the next ten days, with their incessant round of tiresome duties of a nature usually delegated to those in disgrace in the army.

CHAPTER 3

The Battle for Lille

Early in May, 1915, I was enjoying a few hours off duty when I met an artillery officer who was stringing wires from the front-line observation positions to the batteries at the rear.

"Something big coming off?" said I.

"Just that, my son," was the non-committal reply.

This opening seemed interesting, if difficult, and I struck up a precarious conversation with the taciturn old fellow. Two hours of hard work on my part netted the information that the long-delayed battle for Lille was in the making.

For days past our artillery preparations had been active in the extreme. The advance, I gathered, was to be over a line about fifteen hundred yards wide, and from one thousand to twelve hundred artillery pieces were to be concentrated upon that area. According to my oracle, the advance would be simplicity itself, merely a matter of a few hours' artillery fire, and then through the gap and on to Lille.

With these hearty assurances bubbling in my heart, I ran back to the billet and spread the glad news among the boys. Immediately the optimists and the pessimists took sides, and the battle before Lille was fought out according to their respective views. The old-timers were particularly pessimistic, and for good reason. They had been through the Marne, when the Allied artillery was noticeable principally for its absence, and hence word of dominance in artillery-fire was considered too good to be worth the hearing.

At best, they maintained, a battle is merely a matter of luck, and no human brain can forecast the outcome with any degree of accuracy, no matter how elaborate the preparations may be. Furthermore, we had been given to understand that the Germans far outnumbered us, and this fact, coupled with the scepticism concerning our artillery, held sway until the night of May 8, when word came through that on the morrow, Sunday, we would make the long-heralded advance upon Lille.

With the formal news of the impending battle, all scepticism vanished. In its place appeared only optimism and a great eagerness for the onslaught.

Saturday evening, the evening before the battle, we gathered in a shell-proof dugout, where we held high carnival around a bowl of punch. Each lad told his favourite story or sang his favourite song. The health of the British Army and Navy was drunk a score of times. The battle of the coming day was fought and won unquestionably. The spinal cord of the beast was broken. We marched on and on and on into Berlin. Glowing faces grew gay under the mellow, congenial influence of this "Last Supper," as we flippantly called it.

Evening dusk came, we fell into line, and set off on the road which led to "Windy Corners" and to Lille.

At the usual place the German machine-guns picked us up, and for safety's sake we took to the ditch for protection. Across field after field, pitted like the face of the moon, we stumbled, often up to our knees in icy, sticky mud; but about midnight we reached a little wood two miles behind the line, and here we bivouacked for the night.

And here let me offer my very sincere respects to the commander of our platoon, Mr. Findley. He had risen from the ranks and had been decorated with the D.C.M.; and a more conscientious officer I have never known. No matter what his own problems or discomforts, he never forgot "his boys." Around, among us he circulated, now, urging us to be of good cheer, telling of the invincible support of our artillery, tucking waterproof sheets a little tighter, adjusting a haversack for one, a head-rest for another, always helping to make us as comfortable as circumstances would permit. He was self-forgetful, simple, unassuming; always one of us, yet at all times thoroughly respected. And that night was his last night on earth.

The front was as quiet as a sepulchre. From far to the right, however, where the French held the line, came the incessant rumble and crackle of battle. We who knew the code could make out the ebb and flow of the fight from where we lay by the stream of star-shells and multicoloured flares.

No one slept; we lay there relaxed, staring up at the stars. God seemed very near to us that night. When the morning may bring your last day on earth, God becomes a very real and personal being and not some far-off, intangible Deity. No man can go into the trenches and long remain an atheist. He may, and usually does, blaspheme magnificently in the heat of battle, but in the cool quiet of night, when only the sky is overhead, he knows beyond all question that there is a God. I believe that war has converted more men to a true Christianity than any other force of modern times.

War's Christianity is not the sort that sings hymns on public corners. It is a better sort, which serves and gives untiringly.

With the morning came the silence that is proverbial before the storm. Hardly were we out of our waterproof sheets before the ever-present Mr. Findley was among us, passing out good cheer and chocolate. He knew from experience that after such a night none of us could stomach the usual bully beef and biscuit.

At 4:45 a red-capped observation officer appeared from nowhere and clambered up into a tree-top. After an impressive period of time he descended with every evidence of satisfaction. Evidently the stage was set to a nicety and only awaited the actors. Birds were twittering; they seemed oddly out of place. Their chirpings actually annoyed us, so tense were our nerves. A lark shot suddenly heavenward, and was roundly cursed for its efforts.

It was 4:59; one minute more and we would be off and away.

As the hands of my watch touched five the earth shook, the heavens rolled back vast billows of sound, and the air quivered like a living thing. The quiet of a minute before was engulfed in a hell of sound that defied all description. As if a huge hand were manipulating the keys of a tremendous organ, the batteries, massed, some of them wheel to wheel, over that front of fifteen hundred yards, sent out their challenge to the German hosts. From an invisible thing two miles away, the front line burst up before us in a streak of smoke, heaped high, wave on wave, and shot through with green sulphurous fumes, scintillating like waves of heat on a scorching day.

Overhead our aeroplanes roared and hummed, guiding and directing our fire. Pretty things they were, too, oddly birdlike and out of place amid such stern surroundings. In numbers they far outnumbered the German fleet, and successfully held back the Teuton scouts throughout the day.

As we stood drinking in this panorama, the order to advance came through, and we started forward in Indian file, three or four paces apart. Across the terrain we floundered, picking our way around shell-holes and across the debris of former battlefields. There was no fear. In the midst of such terrific noise one becomes only a shrivelled nonentity, incapable of conscious thought.

As we passed in front of our batteries, the concussion doubled, tripled, and quadrupled in intensity, and the roar of a million boiler-shops ripped up and down that line with inhuman exactness and promptitude.

The journey forward was a difficult one, but by 9:30 we were within a few hundred yards of the front line, and German shells were beginning to steal into our ranks. Across a particularly exposed space we ran, but even yet the progress of the battle was a mystery. No authentic word came back; the trenches to the front were merely a vortex of greenish and white smoke.

The Germans were concentrating their fire on the communication trenches and on our reserves. In fact, at this time the men in the front line were comparatively safe. We of the new draft were having our first experience in the gentle art of dodging shells. One learns at a rapid rate under such forced schooling. Within an hour I could tell with a fair degree of accuracy, or so I thought, the shells that bore the message "I want to get you." The shells that would break at a comfortable distance seemed to have another and less ominous sound about them. I was mumbling pretty compliments to myself on my own good judgment when a heavy howitzer-shell burst just a little to my left. Instantly my newly acquired confidence vanished. The fear of God entered my heart, and, like Abraham of old, I fell flat on my face and remained there until the sergeant-major delivered a well-directed kick on a fitting portion of my anatomy.

In addition to the shell-fire, we were now the recipients of the small stuff—pip-squeaks, aero torpedoes, whiz-bangs, and machine-gun-fire. Aside from shell-fire, it is machine-gun-fire that is the most dangerous of all. It traverses up and down your line like a great finger. As it kicks up the dust at your feet your first inclination is to flinch or dodge, and it takes some time before you realize that it is only the harmless bullet that you hear; the one that gets you is as silent as the path to which it leads you.

After two hours of this small stuff we behaved like well-seasoned troops, for we realized fully the utter futility of dodging, and the inevitable fact that our personal bullet would bring no warning spat to guide us.

The pip-squeak, however, continued to annoy me. In fact, I never could get really used to their acrobatics. The father of the pip-squeak is that whistling pinwheel of the fireworks display, which churns upward fifty or a hundred feet, skids, and then explodes in a thousand ill-chosen directions. You can hear a pip-squeak coming, but its crazy course is uncharted. Like a drunken automobile, it careens, now here, now there, and then back here again. The staggering figures following the explosion of a pip-squeak, however, will testify to its effectiveness as an instrument of destruction.

After another half-hour's delay there came another run for it, and we plunged into a communication trench close to the parapeted dressing-station.

Here the horrors of war burst in upon us in all their awful realism. Oh, how a chap's heart goes out to those poor wrecks, tottering, crawling, dragging themselves as best they may to the haven of a first-line dressing-station! You pity them, yes, and you envy them. Their duty is done, their waiting is over, they are going back; your duty is ahead, your fate is uncertain.

They say that the first wounded man you see remains with you throughout your life, and to this day I remember mine with an awful vividness. He was just a kid, and was sitting propped up against the sand-bagged parapet, by the side of a shell-hole filled with slimy water. Off to the left a frog croaked tirelessly, heedless of the hell about him. The wounded man's eyes were closed, and his breath was coming in laboured gasps. His tunic was thrown back, and his chest was as white as a babe's; but just over his heart was an ugly red smudge. Clean through the lung he had it, and as we passed by he went west, quietly and peacefully, like a little child moving in its sleep. There was none of the glory of a dying hero about his passing over the great divide. He had merely done his duty, having been shot on his return from delivering a despatch. Through will power only he held consciousness long enough to crawl back to his superior's dugout to report his duty finished, and then he had passed on.

I was still struggling to throw this picture out of my mind when another chap came limping back, sweat streaming from his face and both hands held to his groin.

"Got a fag, boys?" were his first words. The fag was instantly forthcoming, but someone had to light it for him, for he refused to take his hands from his injured side.

"I got a pretty 'package' here," said he—"shrapnel." That single word "shrapnel" told the entire story, the story of a big gaping wound, and I looked at him curiously.

The London Scottish advance across a captured German trench

"I'm getting awfully tired, lads," were his next words; "I guess I'll sit down." We helped him to a comfortable corner, where he puffed contentedly for a moment upon his borrowed cigarette, and then gasped and died.

Crowding by us in that narrow trench, came an endless line of blood-soaked stretcher cases, some writhing in awful agony, others white and still with head wounds. And down on the quick and the dead alike beat the heat of a noonday sun.

The ghastly harvest streaming by us like a nightmare blanched our faces and made us ache to be over and done with our share.

The waiting—yes, the boys were right—was far more wearing than any fighting that I ever afterward experienced. Perhaps you will not understand the agony of waiting under fire. But have you ever paced the creosoted corridors of a hospital while some one near and dear to you lay upstairs under a skylight, with white-robed, masked figures all about? Do you remember how the minutes crawled past, and how every noise was an explosion? Do you remember pacing the floor of your own room, waiting for the doctor to come down and tell you, "out of danger" or the reverse? Do you remember how the minutes passed then, and how you would have sold your soul itself to have set the clock ahead, if only for one half-hour?

Intensify your feelings of those moments a hundred-fold, and you will have some idea of the agony of waiting in a trench under fire.

By noon our artillery began its barrage fire with renewed fury; but the Germans were still returning shell for shell, and by one o'clock many of our batteries were silenced.

Then the report came back that the Goorkhas, those fierce Indian fighters, had taken the first line German trench; but later in the afternoon we were told that they had been driven out, and still we huddled behind those cursed sand-bags, inactive, burning to be off.

And while we waited, let me just say a word about those same Goorkhas. They are peculiar fellows, as faithful as dogs, fierce as tigers, with a love for their superior officers that is childlike in its simplicity. Many times, when one of their leaders is killed, the thin veneer of civilization which divides the Goorkha from the stone age peels away, and without orders or leaders they will go over the top, *sans* rifle and revolver, armed only with a bowie-knife and a fanatical rage that knows no fear or reasoning.

The bowie-knife is the Goorkha 's favourite weapon, and his expertness with it is uncanny. I have known one to snake away across no-man's-land at night and tap gently on the German parapet. Instantly a helmeted head bobs up in inquiry, a polished blade flashes swiftly, silently, and a German head rolls back into the trench, while a Goorkha snakes back across no-man's-land with a fiendish gleam in his eye, and another story of prowess to tell to the family circle hunched about the meat-pots back home.

At last came the hoped-for order, and up to the second line trenches we filed. But here again we were delayed. Men, some wounded, some stark mad, rushed past us, fruits of high-explosive shelling. A young lieutenant plunged down the trench. He was the sole survivor of a Welsh regiment, and the frightfulness of his losses had quite unseated his reason. Entirely alone in our trench he stood, waving a light cane in one hand and a smoking revolver in the other, and screaming to the sky:

"Where are my men! Good God, where are they! Gone? All gone?" Then he burst into tears.

A sergeant-major who had been wounded in the arm came running up to him.

"Sir," said he, "let me rally your men while you go back to the dressing-station. I'll get the boys together and bring them back to you."

A long and heated argument ensued. The lieutenant was for rallying his own men, but the sergeant-major, a big strapping fellow, with medal ribbons of the Indian Mutiny across his breast, was no mean diplomat, and at last led the lieutenant back and away from the scene from which he alone survived.

We of the Scottish sat huddled together in the trench and saw it all and did nothing. At such times reason sits but lightly, and some of us joked horribly, some sang popular songs in hoarse, unnatural voices, others laughingly made out their last wills and testaments. Fritz and his wonderful war machine came in for their share of complimentary criticism and cursing. The older men recounted many of the ancient trench superstitions—how it is bad luck to light three cigarettes with the same match. For a time premonitions of disaster held the floor as the topic of a heated discussion. A veteran of the Marne swore solemnly that a controlling Deity stood between us and ultimate defeat, and he retold with fervent earnestness how the British retreated for ten days at the Marne, and how on the seventh day a great white sheet interposed itself between our men and the onrushing gray horde of Germans. On the eighth day this sheet took form and shape, and the

Christ looked down upon our troops.

So the minutes passed, but still the order to advance was withheld. Another young lieutenant careened into the trench, bleeding freely from a wound in his arm. Following him came the remnants of his regiment, thirty or forty mud-covered, torn, and tattered men, some limping, others cursing blindly and unceasingly. Squarely in front of us the lieutenant formed his boys up, and then addressed us:

"Well, Jocks, here's what's left of us after half an hour up forward. You know what you can do for us when you go up and over the top this afternoon."

And individually and collectively we swore to avenge his losses, the losses of all England, the losses of France and Belgium, and the losses of humanity.

But the opportunity to avenge was delayed, always delayed. By us streamed an endless chain of war's fresh horrors, constant reminders of our duty still undone. Blood, for us, had become an old story. We were old men, aged immeasurably by six hours in hell's own kitchen, aged by six hours of waiting.

Oh, it is the waiting that tells, my friend. You can fight eternally, you can fight and die, but the horror of waiting is unbearable. You sing, you chatter aimlessly, you count away the seconds and the minutes, while over you stream the Teuton shells, and by you flows the awfulness of war, endless testimony to the efficiency of forty years of Teuton preparation for "*der Tag.*"

At last our major came running up.

"Come on, boys; it's up to us now to finish the job that was started this morning. We're off; hurry up." There were no laggards, and up to the first-line reserve trenches we ran.

It was now 2:30. The attack, *our* attack, was to begin at three. Ahead of us the Black Watch had gone forward. Excitement rose to fever pitch. Our time had come, but no. At 2:50 the brigadier's runner came through, bearing a countermand. If curses could have killed a man, that man would have gone west on the double-quick. After delivering his order he was off to stop the Black Watch.

But he never reached them. A cry went up from down the trench. The Black Watch were going over alone. Utterly regardless of machine-gun-fire, our heads popped up over the parapet. Not four hundred yards away were those chaps. We'd been chatting with them two hours before. They were as cool as on home parade. There was no shouting or yelling, just a clean, collected string of men at double-quick, rifles at their sides, bounding across no-man's-land.

There is something awful in such a sight—eight hundred men headed for sure destruction, and with no chance to help them. We were fascinated by the spectacle. Our captain took in the situation at a glance, and rushed to the brigadier's dugout, where he pleaded and begged to be allowed to go over with them; but already the brigadier had used too many men. The charge of the Black Watch was a mistake; they had failed to receive the countermand. At some place between us and them the despatch-bearer had fallen, and eight hundred men went with him.

It was perhaps seven or eight hundred yards from our trenches to the German line, nearly half a mile, and over this space went the "Ladies from Hell," as the Germans call the Scottishers. Even the Hun, with all his horrors, seemed stunned by their advance. The shell-fire slackened visibly, and only the machine-gun bullets remained to remind us of our personal danger.

That day, it is estimated, the Germans had a machine-gun for every five yards of front. A machine-gun can pour out six hundred to six hundred and fifty bullets per minute. It was into this hail of steel that our friends, the Black Watch, plunged.

A hush fell over our lines. Half-way across, and only a scant six hundred of the original eight hundred remained. Another hundred yards took their toll, another, and then another. Then they came to the dummy trench, some twenty-five or thirty yards in front of the German first line. This dummy trench was filled with barbed wire, and a rivulet had been turned into it for the occasion. Two hundred men reached that trench, two hundred men went into it, but only one hundred crossed it and dashed on over the last few yards.

Then they were gone from sight. Sixty of the eight hundred had reached the German trench. It was all over; but, no! Their signaller is on the German parapet calling for help, and he is calling for the Scottish, for us! And we had orders to stay! God, man, it was awful! During those minutes of agony I grew old. The signaller had barely finished his message when he was shot down, and we sank back into our trench, dumb with the horror of it all. That stretch of no-man's-land, dotted with still or writhing figures, swam before my eyes.

A cry went up. They were coming back. Yes, sure enough, twenty-five or thirty of them, divested of all equipment, were running back toward us.

Then the heart that actuates the Teuton army showed itself for what it was. Running across no-man's-land came thirty brave lads who had fought a brave fight and lost. They were entitled to the honour of any soldier, be he friend or foe; but do you think they got it from the Hun? They did not.

Here they came running toward us, the last of eight hundred. Behind them you could hear the crack of a German machine-gun going into action. Like pigeons at a pigeon shoot they were trapped, but without half the chance of escape that we give the bird. Away over to the left I saw McDonald stagger and collapse. On across that fleeing line of heroes traversed that German machine-gun. One by one the boys dropped until not one remained. *KULTUR!*

Our men at first were dazed; they didn't believe their own eyes. It was impossible barbarism. Thirty men entitled to all the scant privileges of war had been shot down like gutter-dogs. Then, as the reality broke in upon us, a cry went up, and a demand to go over and avenge that wholesale murder. If discipline was ever put to the test it was then. It seemed for a minute as though nothing could restrain that wild rage, that thirst for vengeance, that desire to rid ourselves of the hideous sense of impotence in the face of such horrors. But the months of training told, and with a few steadying words the officers kept control of the situation.

The day was done. Our artillery had failed to sever the German barbed wire sufficiently, and as our men cut away at it they had been shot down like rats. Lille was still to be won.

The artillery of both sides still worked away intermittently, but the work was done, though far from finished.

Like a continuous bad dream the wounded drifted past us, but we did not see or hear them. It was out yonder, in no-man's-land, that we lived, out there where our men lay kicking their last, under the heat of an afternoon sun. But even yet the day had not completed its tale of horror for us.

A random howitzer-shell shrieked overhead. Closer and closer it came. There was a flash, a stunning concussion, and our Mr. Findley rolled out of the smoke. A dozen of us rushed up to him and tried to stop the flow of blood from the wound in his side. He was in frightful agony. Beads of icy sweat stood out on his forehead, and his eyes burned like coals. Near him lay three other boys of the London Scottish. He saw them, and motioned to us to stop in our work.

"Don't mind me, fellows," he said; "look after those poor chaps over there. I'll be all right—soon."

At this juncture Mr. Steadman, our commanding officer, rushed up and ordered a stretcher; but poor Findley was gone. They got him back of the lines all right, but somewhere on the rough road between there and the hospital at Bethune he went west, and as he went the British Empire lost a man among men, a Christian of war's awful making.

Volunteers were asked for to go out into no-man's-land that night and bring in the wounded. My pal Nichols and I stepped forward, as did the vast majority of our company. We were fortunate enough to be selected.

Just as we were leaving for the rear, another shell found us, and ten of our number felt its bite. I knew them all intimately. Eight of them never reached the hospital. Callendar had a leg off, and one of the others had had his head blown off. Three fell where they stood. I thought they had fainted, but later I learned that they had been killed by the concussion.

From this scene we stretcher-bearers went back for final instructions to the dressing-station; and, oh, the horror of that dressing-station! Long rows of wounded, mud- and blood-bespattered wrecks, some groaning softly, others quiet, still others puffing cigarettes. A canvas curtain flashed back, and three surgeons were revealed under the oil-lamp.

Comparatively few operations are performed at the dressing-station; only when seconds divide life from death does the dressing-station do aught but temporary bandaging. From this first station you are sent to a station farther back, where your wounds are minutely examined, and you are marked for Blighty or for a field hospital, as the case may indicate.

At nine, as darkness fell, we went out into no-man's-land for the first time since we had come to France. Darkness after a battle is a pleasing thing. It hides the gruesome details that day lays bare in horrid profusion. After the day the night seemed quiet, and we went from form to form seeking those in whom the spark of life still clung. As star-shells or flares sputtered upward we fell prone, and imitated the still figures about us. Between flares we worked feverishly.

I will not describe that night. It beggars all description. In the heat of battle you forget the horror of it, but in the stillness of night it flashes back over you in a mighty flood.

I remember, I will always remember, those endless trips to and from the dressing-station—now with a chap crying softly to himself, like a little baby, now with one lying limp and voiceless. Those pleading eyes that looked up at us as we passed will haunt me till Berlin bows.

"For God's sake, boys, take me in! I've got a little wife and a kiddy at home—a kiddy with big blue eyes; yes, fellows, blue eyes."

"Oh, boys, water! God, give me water!"

"A cigarette, men. I'm going west soon, and I've got to have a cigarette before I start."

Such are the echoes of battle; but it is the still form, shapeless, sombre, that raises no echoes, that calls the loudest to you. How many such forms lay out in no-man's-land that night I do not know. I do not even want to know. It is enough to remember that call:

"For God's sake, boys, take me in! I've got a little wife and kiddy at home—a kiddy with big blue eyes."

All night we rushed back and forth from one hell to the other; but as day dawned we reported for the last time. Half of the fellows who had gone out on that errand of mercy that night remained out there among the other dead and dying, victims of the machine-gun-fire, which sweeps up and down no-man's-land by night and day.

Our battalion, on its return from the trenches, had been billeted fifteen miles back of the lines, and as the sun peered over the red rim of the world we trudged homeward to this billet. Those were the longest fifteen miles I ever covered. The excitement was gone, but the horror still remained. The reaction had set in, and Nichols and I floundered along those interminable miles of road, as silent as the grave which we had left.

We found our company in a long shed, and we tumbled in among them, worn to the point of breaking. Two hours of unconsciousness, and we were wakened for roll-call.

Roll-call after a battle! It is the saddest of all scenes. As each man's name is called the company listens. There is a silence—gone, another one gone, another. God! Roll-call after a battle is almost as bad as the battle itself. You relive it all, you see that shell strike five yards from your dearest friend; Jim, Pete, Tommy—all gone, and you remember how they went.

We had but a scant eight hundred left from our battalion of near-ly four thousand! That is roll-call after a battle. Thirty-two hundred names were called out with no answer.

We of the London Scottish alone had clicked five hundred and fifty-four of our original one thousand, and we had been mere re-serves and had seen none of the real fighting.

The horror of it all is indescribable. We were stunned by our losses. In the heat of action we had hardly realized their immensity. We had seen individual cases, but here the vast panorama of horror was unrolled before us. The officers realized our sensations and set us free, and we rambled over to an orchard, a cherry orchard, in full bloom.

From far off came the boom of the firing line, but thank God that was past for the time. We read letters from home, and wrote replies; we chatted vaguely, and rested, preparatory to the next assault on the German lines.

CHAPTER 4

The Man in the Blue Jeans

As the afternoon wore on and our letters were duly written and censored, several of us wandered over to an estaminet.

An *estaminet* is one of those denatured *cafés*, found far behind the lines, at which soft drinks and light refreshments may be purchased from the peasantry of the community.

This *estaminet* was filled to overflowing with the fortunates who had survived the battle of the previous day. Here we met the Guards Regiment which had gone over the top, only to retreat in the face of the withering Teuton machine-gun fire. I say we met the regiment, but what we actually met was a scant tenth of it, for the rest were either back yonder in no-man's-land or in one or more of the field hospitals.

For an hour or two the battle for Lille was refought. The reason for its failure was sought out and found a hundred times, and at a back table a group of Frenchmen listened in silence.

Then, during one of those lulls which sometimes come over even the noisiest of gatherings, one of these taciturn Frenchmen sprang to his feet. In broken, but excited, English he denounced the Scottish and all we stood for. In fact, his denunciation covered quite an extensive territory, for it encompassed the whole of England and Ireland and most of the colonies. He cursed us roundly as "slackers" who had failed to accomplish our objective.

Immediately the room was in an uproar. An old lady, who was the proprietress, rushed in and added her shrieks to the general clamour.

For two or three minutes it looked like a riot or a murder or both. But, fortunately for the discomfited Frenchmen, saner heads took hold of the situation. The hot-headed native who had forgotten himself was escorted none too gently from the *estaminet*, to be persuaded verbally, but effectively, of the error of his ways in a less public spot.

The old proprietress apologized to us in her most elegant and effusive English, and then the meeting broke up. We were momentarily too disgusted to continue to enjoy French hospitality.

Do not misunderstand me. We Tommies like the French, we thoroughly love them, but occasionally one of these fiery Frenchmen, brooding over multitudinous hardships, will burst loose, and, although his eruption is harmless enough to us of more stoical English stock who understand, each such outburst leaves a temporary wound. But in a few hours our anger wears off, and we laugh the matter down and forget it, along with the rest of our manifold troubles of trenchdom.

On returning to the billet that evening, word was passed around that there was a spy in our midst, who had been active in obtaining information and in forwarding it with remarkable despatch to the German lines.

Suspicion had been directed to a workman in one of the adjoining fields. Innocent enough he seemed, to all outward appearances,—short, stocky, dressed in blue jeans about ten sizes too big for him. To the casual observer he was a hard-working French peasant, and naught else. There was, however, something a little unusual about him. It was perfectly natural that a Frenchman should take some interest in our goings and comings, but there is a point at which legitimate interest stops, and this man in the blue jeans had exceeded these bounds of decent curiosity. Each morning as we went out on route marches, regardless of the hour or weather, we observed him out there digging in the field, always digging. Apparently this gentleman belonged to the Night Owl fraternity, for he was up long before the larks and retired but very little before moon-up.

Such diligence, even for a French peasant, is remarkable. Even so, he might have passed without exciting suspicion, had he not on one occasion been observed to pull out a pair of binoculars from the depths of his jeans and scan the horizon and the varied actions of our troops.

Now, binoculars are not generally found on French peasants. Neither does a French peasant habitually use chance binoculars industriously, and then jot down notes in a little book. Yet the man in the blue jeans had been observed engaged in both of these unusual pastimes.

Obviously, the case required diplomatic handling. In the first place, there was danger of hurting the peasant's feelings, should he prove to be but an innocent observer who by sheer chance had come into possession of a pair of binoculars. As you can guess, the feelings of a Frenchman are somewhat easily injured, especially by false suspicions of loyalty, and, as we had informal orders to keep on the sunny side of the French people, both collectively and individually, our commanding officer desired that the man in the blue jeans be given the most cordial treatment possible under the circumstances.

Sergeant McFarland, who was something of a linguist and particularly adept at the French language, was appointed *Sherlock Holmes* of the occasion. Promptly at six o'clock in the morning, he walked leisurely down the road which ran alongside the field in which the peasant worked. The sergeant's air was one of great unconcern. To all outward appearances he might have been a gentleman out for a stroll, viewing his estate.

From the neighbouring bushes we watched his progress. Quite casually he observed the peasant, and engaged him in idle conversation. The weather was thoroughly covered. Past, present, and future battles were discussed, all quite casually, of course, and then we observed the two walking down the road together toward battalion headquarters. Later we found that our sergeant had invited the peasant to have a neighbourly drink with him at the *estaminet*.

It had been arranged that if both of them walked by headquarters, real suspicions had been fastened upon the peasant and he was to be quietly nabbed on his arrival. In order to make the kidnapping as genteel as possible, the sergeant invited him to step into headquarters, but the peasant was wise beyond his day and age, and protested vehemently.

Immediately a couple of our boys, who had been waiting for just such a protest, carried him in bodily, and he was immediately quizzed in regard to his past, present, and probable future.

It was found that he was a Frenchman all right, but for a long period had been in the employ of the Wilhelmstrasse. He was of German-French parentage, born in Alsace of a German father and a French mother. Of course, under these circumstances, the German parentage predominated, and the subtle doctrines of the *Kaiser* had been inculcated in him from his earliest youth, until now, half French though he was, he was a willing worker for that great fetish of all Germans, *der Vaterland*. Pending further investigation, this Germanized native of Alsace was sent back under escort to divisional headquarters.

The following day the field in which he had been so industriously digging for several weeks was thoroughly searched, and in a little straw-pile near a stable, a complete heliograph outfit was discovered. With this he had been relaying his information to a German observation balloon not many miles away.

After observing the action taken by your country under somewhat similar circumstances, I am led to believe that had this man been caught in the same act on the parade ground of West Point, he would have been interned as a dangerous character. But over there in France, where the bodies of civilized humanity are pushing the daisies up, there is no room for dangerous characters. Over there you are either for us, or you are against us. There is no neutral ground. You cannot be dangerous and live. In fact, it is wiser not to be even *suspected* of dangerous inclinations.

Circumstantial though the evidence against this spy may have been, the Flanders front had little shrift for him, and a few mornings later his back was against a stone wall and the firing squad was in front.

In and about this little village we rested for four days, and much rivalry was provoked by the village beauty. Every village in France, you know, has its "beauty." When the number of soldiers sufficiently outweighs the number of girls, *every* girl becomes a recognized village beauty. But in this particular instance there was one lassie who so far outshone the others that she was unanimously accepted as the logical Queen of the May.

I remember her well. She was tall and dark, with the sparkling eyes and beautiful carriage of the typical young French peasant girl.

Hardly had we been in the village an hour before discussion was rife as to who would be her escort for the period of our stay. There was a great deal of good-natured skirmishing for her smiles; in fact, the neighbouring *estaminet* was well-nigh forsaken in favour of this fair damsel's dwelling. She was running no *estaminet*, but it was remarkable how many soldiers found her farmhouse much cooler and more attractive than the established *estaminet* a few rods farther down the street. I think before the day was over the entire platoon had called, quite informally, of course, at her home and begged for a cup of coffee, some bread and butter, or for almost anything that would give an excuse to linger in her presence. The prices which she received for such small favours would make your Mr. Hoover wail with anguish.

I myself was one of the aspirants for this fair maid's affections, and, thinking to steal a march on the rest of the platoon, I went over there at dusk one night, with a very definite plan worked out for gaining her company during the balance of the evening. By devious paths I arrived at her farm, and was just going around the barn when I ran into and nearly knocked over an officer, engaged in a similar flank attack from the rear.

Evening is the favourite time with officers for affairs of the heart. The reasons are obvious. An officer is not popularly supposed to be prone to such airy fancies. Some of them feel that it would lower them in the estimation of their men, were they to be so much as suspected of playing the gay Lothario. Hence, from the standpoint of safety, as well as for the romantic glamour which sifts down of an evening, it is in this dusky season that the young officer of the army must do his billing and cooing.

Knowing this full well, I required no engraved invitation from the officer to retire. This I did in bad order, and the officer, by force of superior authority, became the acknowledged escort of the lady fair throughout the balance of our stay.

From this village we went to Givenchy. You have heard long before this, perhaps, of the famous brick-fields of Givenchy. A few days before our arrival these brick-fields had been the scene of a bloody battle in which three of our regiments had been engaged.

The brick-fields, or kilns, were arranged in long rows twenty or thirty yards apart. It took our forces an entire day to capture the first line of kilns, and the better part of a week was consumed in cleaning the Germans out of the vicinity. It was in this locality that we were to stay until the new draft arrived from England to fill our ranks, depleted by the catastrophe before Lille.

As we marched up, the men whom we were to relieve were just returning from the front-line trenches, and, during a brief halt, we had an opportunity to exchange the time of day with them.

I well remember talking with one young chap who had seen his first action at these brick-kilns, and I asked him how things were going. He said:

"To be truthful, it's hell up there. I never realized the awfulness of war before, and do you know, I don't mind the fighting a bit; it is before and after the fighting that hurts. Before the fighting you are waiting to be shot, and after the fighting you are waiting to bring in the fellows who *were* shot, and you hear and see them all about you. Give me fighting every time, but let me skip before and after."

Givenchy was just a little hamlet, with few points of interest aside from the brick-fields and the remains of a house which had served both Germans and French as headquarters when the battle-lines swayed back and forth.

I, along with several other curiosity-seekers, went over to the ruins of the *château*. It was an immense place, the centre of a vast French estate. Even yet, about the courtyard and garden, were the remains of trenches and many gruesome relics of the hand-to-hand fighting that had taken place there. One-half of the house and a liberal portion of the adjoining territory were nothing but a tremendous hole half-filled with greenish water and debris,—the work of a French mine.

Mining is one of the most hazardous occupations carried on in trenchland. England is fortunate in having a tremendous source of supply in her Welsh coal-miners. These men are extremely quick, and are daring to the point of rashness.

The mines, or "saps" as they are commonly called, are tunnelled fifty to two hundred yards. Speed is a necessary requisite in this work. The dirt is carried away on little tramcars far enough back so that suspicion will not be excited on the opposing side. The saps are of varied size. Some are only large enough to crawl into, while others are four or five feet high. In mining the English have very much the edge on the Germans. The Welsh miners work with almost incredible swiftness, scratching ahead like dogs in a burrow. They seem to have an intuitive knowledge of direction and the general nature of the ground through which they are digging. This last is important, because to strike a stone with a pick may disclose the progress of operations to a German listening, his ear to the ground, in a fire-trench or similar sap not many yards away.

These miners work in shifts, much as they do back under the sea at the tip end of England. The mining of Messines Ridge bears ample testimony to their expertness. When a mine is exploded, the earth belches up skyward in a great wave. You have doubtless seen pictures of a naval battle, and you will remember the action of the water when it is struck by a shell. Under the urge of a high-explosive mine, solid earth and rock behave in much the same manner. You can literally see the edges of the earth bend and rush upward into the air. Then, all about the fringe of dirt and smoke, you see the heavier objects dropping down.

In the mining of the *château* it was a race against time, as both the Germans and French were mining, the Frenchmen under the Germans. The French got there first, and as their mine leaped up into the air report has it that upward of two thousand German reserves, who had just come up from their billets, went west.

The region about Givenchy had formerly been a mining district, and the fields were bare, except for the houses, wrecks of which cluttered the battle-line for many miles on each side. To our right was the shaft-head of a coal mine slightly behind our lines, and the Germans shelled this constantly to prevent our working it. It was here that I had my first experience with the German *minenwerfer*, as they ponderously called it. Quick-witted Tommy long ago dubbed this particular shell, "Minnie." It is about as nasty a thing as I ever had to deal with. The shells that whistle high above your head are directed at the artillery behind the lines, and they worry you not at all. But "Minnie," which Fritz shoots from his trench-mortar, is an exceedingly nasty lady. It is a large shell that explodes with a tremendous noise and concussion. I have known men to be killed outright by the concussion alone. The shells trundle through the air, and you can actually see them coming. This gives you time to dodge down into a dugout. But familiarity always breeds contempt, and we boys, after a few days' acquaintance with them, took to shooting at these "Minnies," much as though they were clay pigeons.

Such familiarity should not be taken to indicate the ineffectiveness of the *minenwerfer*. When one of them lands correctly, which is not very frequently, it means a tremendous lot of pick-and-shovel work for several hours. Where a "Minnie" hits, the landscape is badly shattered, and a big gap in the trench and parapet must be filled in double-quick time.

We had been at Givenchy but a few hours when the new draft of four hundred and fifty men from England, fresh from a training camp, came up to fill the pitiful gaps in our ranks. With the new draft came new friends, and old friends, too.

Home! How good it seemed to hear from it again! We were like boys returning to school after a vacation, and we swapped stories of home- and trench-life unceasingly, just as those other veterans, many of whom were now dead, had swapped these same stories with us upon our arrival not many months before.

As luck would have it, a chap whom I had known back home came with this draft. He told me that he had almost given up hope of ever reaching the firing-line, owing to his lack of skill with a rifle. Three times he had been turned down for poor musketry, and he rejoiced at his arrival in trenchdom as though it were a long-postponed theatre party.

Under the spell of the trenches friendships were quickly made, and such friendships bring with them a far deeper and truer fellowship than any friendship formed under less trying circumstances. There is remarkably little discord either in the trenches or behind the lines. Fellowship reigns supreme. Of course we have our little squabbles, but they are squabbles and nothing more. There is endless bantering, but when the chaffing reaches too white a heat for comfort, more sober heads interpose and stop the gathering storm before it becomes unmanageable.

After a day or two of rest we advanced to the firing line in the cool of evening. It was a short, uphill walk. Lights were out, there was no talking, and we had strict orders to guard against any clinking of accoutrements. Reserves coming up are a pet bull's-eye for the Teuton artillery, and the utmost secrecy and quiet must be maintained for safe-conduct. At five hundred yards, on a quiet night, the noise of one bayonet striking against another may mean the beginning of a battle. Under such circumstances the carelessness of a pal, however slight, becomes a crime of tremendous proportions. Your nerves are all a tingle. You almost fear to breathe.

That night I had my first spell at listening-post duty. In this sector we had three listening-posts about one hundred yards apart. The first extended out to within seventy-five yards of the German trench; the second reached to within fifty yards; and the third was separated from the hungry hand of the Hun by scarcely more than thirty yards.

It was to this third post that I was ordered. Listening-post duty, especially in an advanced position such as mine, is no sinecure. There is some comfort in being in a trench and knowing that you have full permission to fire whenever the spirit so moves, but out in an advanced listening-post you have strict and absolute orders to fire under no circumstances whatsoever.

There are two men in such a position. One keeps watch, while the other stands ready to run back with any news of an impending attack. My particular listening-post was far out beyond our own barbed wire, and was supposed to be concealed. Without exerting myself in the least, I could hear the Germans talking in their trench. It rather amused me that night, the way the patrols came up every hour to see that we were on the job and not asleep. I couldn't have slept if my life had hung upon it.

It was a new sector, and in no-man's-land there still remained a patch of grass here and there and a few ghostlike stalks of waving wheat. Fifty times that night I identified one of these stalks as the advancing German army. I had "Boche fever," and I had it right. It really wasn't my fault either, because a certain fresh corporal had told me in great confidence that same evening how he had it on good authority that the Germans were going to come over at eleven o'clock.

Eleven o'clock was my turn to watch and the other fellow's to run back, in case the Germans should come. At such a time, of the two horns of the dilemma, the chap who runs back has the best horn. The one who stays in the advance listening-post has 999 chances to 1 of being put on intimate terms with a German bomb or bayonet. As he is forbidden to fire, no matter what the price of silence, all he can do is to stand his ground and trust that the Germans will overlook him. The Huns, however, are very thorough, and seldom are they guilty of such errors of omission.

With this story of impending attack churning in my head, you can imagine my sensations as I took my turn and watched my timepiece tick away the hours from eleven o'clock on. But my promised Teuton advance did not materialize, and the cold sweat dried in the chill breeze of morning.

At three o'clock every one "stands to." That is, at this hour every one must be up on the firing-step ready for action, with rifle loaded, safety-catch thrown back, and bayonet in place. Three o'clock in the morning has a neck-and-neck race with dusk as the popular moment for German attacks, and cruel experience has taught the Allied armies to be ready at this hour.

The next day came rumours of a proposed trench raid. Trench raids are one means of obtaining information in regard to opposing forces. The raiders sneak out from a sap-head or advance listening-post and, if possible without being discovered, endeavour to jump into a section of the opposite trench and drag a luckless Fritz or two back to their own lines. The object of this game is to win without firing a shot. So far as I know this object has never been attained. Either going or coming or in the middle of the raid you are discovered and, as a result, trench raids are a prolific source of casualties.

Service in such a raid is usually a matter of volunteering, and that evening, when volunteers were called for, I stepped forward and was chosen, along with fifty-two other chaps who were anxious to experience the zenith of trench excitement.

It was a deucedly rotten night. A nasty, cold drizzle had settled down, and everything was afloat. The tall, dank grass between our lines and the German trenches was wetter than the rain itself. Occasionally a flare forced its way up through the mist, but it gave little light, owing to the vapour in the atmosphere. On the preceding night our patrols had been out and had cut a lane through the German barbed wire that would permit us to go forward about four abreast.

Since quiet in going, coming, and execution of a raid is essential, few firearms were taken along. Our decorations that evening consisted largely of long, ugly trench-knives and "knuckle-dusters" or "brass knuckles" as they are known in the parlance of the second-story man.

Before setting out we were stripped of all marks of identification, such as regimental insignia, etc., so that the capture of any of us might not disclose information of value to the enemy.

While the trenches at this point were within seventy-five yards of each other, we took a diagonal course from one of the sap-heads and had about one hundred yards to go across no-man's- land. Our objective was a German sap-head at which was posted a machine-gun. It was our privilege to enter this sap-head, capture the occupants, and bring them back, along with their machine-gun and, incidentally, ourselves. The prisoners were to be brought back alive, if possible, that they might be subjected to the "third degree" and any and all information in regard to the opposing forces wrung from them.

A code of signals had been arranged, so that our progress might be intelligently guided by the officer in command. Such signals consist of taps on the ground. The commanding officer is in the centre. One tap means "go forward." This is passed down each side of the line until it reaches the end. It is then passed back. When the officer hears the tap come back, he knows that all are fully informed of the movement. Two taps mean "halt after fifty paces," and three taps mean "go at them."

Half way across we halted for a final adjustment of our line, and then prepared to rush the trench.

The machine-gun emplacement was just behind the German barbed wire entanglement and extended out from the Teuton line proper about thirty-five yards. As we reached the breach in the barbed wire we halted, took a deep breath, and at a given signal rushed forward as quietly as haste would permit. Dividing to the left and right, some of us jumped into the trench midway between the emplacement and the German line. Others jumped into the emplacement itself. Here we found three Germans. One of them was bayoneted, being too unruly for convenient capture. The other two were dragged back without ceremony to our own lines. Concerning the action at the machine-gun emplacement I know little, for I was one of ten who jumped into the sap in order to prevent the German lines from sending assistance to their men at the sap-head.

Of course the raid was overheard in the quiet of the evening, and no sooner had the first shot been fired than all of no-man's-land became a living hell of bullets and almost as bright as day with a multitude of flares from the German trenches.

I vaguely remember two Germans—the trenches permit but two men to advance abreast—rushing down upon us two Scottish, who stood between the Germans and their friends at the machine-gun emplacement. We did not know what was going on behind us. It was our duty to fend off all reinforcements from the firing line. I braced myself for the shock of attack. Somebody threw a bomb, and the blackness in front of me collapsed and sank down. Behind him came a towering mass of onrushing, helmeted forms—myriads of them, apparently—and I lunged forward blindly with my bayonet.

If I should describe the action of the next two minutes, I would be lying, because I do not know exactly what did happen. I remember lunging repeatedly, missing sometimes and sometimes not. There was no room or time for conscious parrying, but when the signal came for us to retreat the four of us who survived the action in the sap-trench sprang over the edge and crawled back for our trenches, like snakes bound for their holes at the break of day.

On our return we found our objective had been gained—two German prisoners were there, big as life. But they proved expensive luxuries, for of the fifty-three who went out on this trench raid, only nine returned. Some thirty-five had been wounded or killed, and the others had been captured. Five or six of the boys lay out in no-man's-land for twenty-four hours before our stretcher-bearers could reach them.

Yet with all its dangers a trench raid has a rare element of excitement. The danger comes not so much in the raid itself, as on the return journey. In going over and in the actual attack you have the element of surprise in your favour. Fritz in his sap-head may be dozing. At best, he is far outnumbered. The moments of real action are few and short. In fact, the entire raid from start to finish does not consume more than two or three minutes, but it is two or three minutes of the most intense fighting, where individual initiative comes in for its own and just reward.

I imagine that your American troops will be particularly successful at trench-raid work. I am sure that they will far outshine Fritz, who is a methodical being as a rule and little given to individual thought, apparently. When he has orders to guide him, he runs like some automaton; he is uncanny. But in trench raids, when it is man for man and the devil take the hindmost, Fritz is rather stunned by the suddenness of it all and is more than likely to be captured without much show of resistance, in which, perhaps, he is wise.

CHAPTER 5

Nichols Goes West

Very shortly our battalion was ordered back to Bethune.

We set off late one night and covered the twelve kilometres by early dawn of the following day. There we found the billets to which we had been assigned were chock full of sleeping soldiery. Our commanding officer and the officer in charge of the billet exchanged numerous uncomplimentary remarks as a result of the mix-up. But in war, as in peace, possession is nine points of the law, and we had to seek other billets elsewhere.

By the best of good fortune we located one of those old French barns which are two or three times as large as the barn with which you are familiar. The floors are tile, and along the sides are great beams covered with hay. These hay-covered beams are at a premium among the boys, and the first-comers invariably clamber up to them and usurp them for their own.

Little time was spent in sleeping, however, for we were once more near to civilization. Accompanied by six or eight of my comrades, I drew what pay was coming to me and went into Bethune proper, where my $2.50 quickly disappeared into the outstretched hands of the genial French populace.

After a brief but cheering hour of fellowship at an estaminet, we started across town with the avowed intention of finding Mr. Findley's grave. The last we had seen of Mr. Findley had been at the battle for Lille. We knew that he had been buried in the military cemetery at Bethune. Following directions, we went through the town and out on the far side, where in the distance we saw the civilian cemetery stretching out before us.

The old caretaker at the gate examined us severely, but after much gesticulation our mission was explained to him, and he swung back the heavy bronze gateway as though it were a duty second only in importance to that of the Premier.

This was my first sight of a French cemetery, and I was struck with the simple, unpretentious manner in which the French decorate the graves of their dead. Humble little marble crosses were everywhere. Occasionally a more pretentious vault loomed up. Pictures of Christ were all about. On the more humble graves were bouquets of waxed flowers under glass cases.

Through this depressing scene we strode, realizing full well how our costumes jangled with the peaceful surroundings. On the far side the military cemetery adjoined the civilian cemetery. There was no mistaking it, for, as we came to the edge of the formal civilian plot, God's military acre stretched out before us on either side as far as the eye could reach, mute testimony to the efficiency of *kultur*.

The military cemetery was a sharp contrast to the civilian resting-place we had left behind us. Row on row of plain deal crosses swept away into the distance and over the slight rise of ground, apparently endlessly.

To our right were a number of rows of newly-dug graves. To the reader not familiar with war, or unhardened to its practical side, the method of burying even our honoured dead will come with something of a shock. Very few of them have a single grave. Instead, long trenches are dug, the sides stepping up like mammoth steps on the Pyramids of Egypt. In the lowest trench rests a single rough casket; on top of it and on each side, on the next higher step, are other caskets; and so on upward until the trench is filled.

In quiet times, when there is little fighting, these trenches are dug in preparation for the sterner days to come, and you will always see the ends of a pile of rough boxes jutting out into daylight, awaiting new arrivals before the earth is thrown over them.

Yet in all its immensity this cemetery represented only a fraction of our Allied dead. It is only those who reach the hospital to die who are formally buried in such a cemetery. Those who are fortunate, or unfortunate, enough to die a sudden death out in no-man's-land, or in trench-land, are hastily buried in a shallow scooped-out grave hard by, and lucky, indeed, are they if so much as a plain cross decorates their last resting-place.

It was down row after row of these polygamous graves that we strode, hunting for that little cross which would mark the grave of our Mr. Findley. We knew that we would recognize it, for we had been told that it was set apart from its fellows by the red Saint Andrew's Cross of Scotland. And so at last we came upon it.

At such moments nothing is said and nothing is done. Man and life and all life's petty vicissitudes become as little things in the face of the grim reaper. About Mr. Findley's grave we stood, hatless and wordless, silent tributes to this great Christian of war's making and to the cause for which he fought and gave his all.

Then, instinctively, we bent and each gathered a handful of pebbles. With them we outlined the approximate boundaries of Mr. Findley's grave, not knowing then whether he rested directly underneath or two or three layers down. But it seemed only right that a man who had given so much, both in life and in death, should have his grave set apart, if only by a little, from those surrounding him.

We finished our work of reverence and departed, walking silently through the military cemetery and then on through the civilian cemetery by which we had entered. As we passed, we met a company of French women. There were five of them. One was evidently the mother, while the others may have been her daughters or near of kin. They were of the peasant class, roughly dressed, with wooden sabots. The old mother cried incessantly, while the younger women busied themselves nervously in decorating one of the graves with the simple offerings afforded by their scanty income. An ordinary little jam-pot was upturned. Within it was an inscription, scribbled, perhaps, by the village *padre*, awaiting only the time when the family's savings would be sufficient to warrant a more pretentious record of their loved one's life and death.

And over it all, like the bass notes of a great organ, played the roar of distant gun-fire, an incessant salute to those who had gone on never to return.

Saddened by our grim mission of the afternoon, we felt in need of another visit to an estaminet on our return journey. By pooling our resources we managed to collect sufficient funds for a brief, a very brief, stay. One of the boys, who was more familiar with the *estaminets* of Bethune than the rest of us, led the way to one where he assured us the most beautiful woman in France waited on table. In my estimation his judgment was nearly correct, but, after all, when you have been in the trenches for three or four weeks, a feminine face takes on a charm never seen in civilian life. Unquestionably, however, this little waitress was of no ordinary clay. She was a petite little thing, fully experienced in the proper handling of British soldiery. Though we had but little, we spent our last cent. If we had had ten times as much, she and her wily ways would have won it all from us just as easily.

I am in much accord with Mark Twain, who says that the French do not understand their own language. Certainly, in ordering a meal the French have no more idea of what we Britishers desire than have we of the proper word to describe it. The usual order at a French *estaminet* is the French for "four-egg omelet." This preference for omelets, and particularly for a "four-egg omelet," will be understood when I tell you that the French phrase sounds much like "omelet with a cat roof." When all else fails, by a simple process of memory "omelet with a cat roof" brings the desired results. Hence it has become the standard meal of the British soldier seeking a change of diet at a French *estaminet*.

While returning to the billet we met a company of troops coming from the living hell at Ypres. Like all troops, they were "grousing" and complaining about everything, from the stars above to the earth beneath. They were leaving the hottest part of the line for one of the more quiet sections. This they felt to be ample cause for complaint. I do not know, but probably their rations had been unusually good, their officers unusually considerate, and the mail service from home unusually liberal; hence nothing remained worth complaining about except this very satisfactory transfer. They made the most of it.

Immediately upon our return to Bethune that afternoon our battalion was transferred to a position nearer the firing-line. As we marched out of the town the last bakery shop was bought out of all supplies, and we marched on, laden down equally with equipment and delicacies of French concoction.

It may seem odd to you that we could spend all our money at a French *estaminet* and yet have more for the luxury of a French bakery. This is easily understood when I explain that one soldier's credit on leaving a town is perfectly good for another. Neither may ever return, and hence money on the way up to the firing-line is one of the most valueless of all possessions. When leaving the firing-line, however, and when approaching a town, money takes on added stature and girth. It so happened that we were leaving the luxuries of life for the stern realities of the trench, and those with money about them found it valueless, since there was nothing on which to spend it. Therefore they much preferred to lend it and thereby provide for a rainy day to come,—should that day ever arrive.

Up to the extreme right of the British line we went, replacing a number of French troops who had been withdrawn in preparation for a drive in the Champagne district, a prelude to the Battle of Champagne and later to Verdun.

It was now dark as the proverbial coal-hole. About a mile or a mile and a half back of the line proper we entered the communication trench, and for seemingly endless hours we tramped on, turn after turn, endlessly and always. A mile and a half as the crow flies is likely to be three miles or more in a communication trench.

Coming back all the time were men laden down with this or that, and others were going to relieve them or to replace them, for no man can leave the front line without another coming to take his place. The front line must always be filled.

As we drew nearer and nearer, occasional flares which shot up higher than their brothers gave us a vague hint of our general direction, but when they went out the night seemed blacker than before, and east and west and north and south became mere figures of speech. Under a huge chateau we went, like New Yorkers on their way to work. Here the trench branched out to the left and to the right, and, owing to the darkness, part of our battalion lost touch with the balance and wound its way down the left-hand trench.

We did not discover this until we were almost at the front line, when we had to return and find our lost brethren. We located them swearing away in the left-hand trench, which, after endless plodding, they had discovered to be a blind alley.

Fifty yards from the front line we encountered the French regiment returning. No more foreign-looking body of men have I ever seen. They were laden down with odd-shaped packs that, in the darkness, gave them a wholly unnatural size and shape. Their excitement over leaving the danger zone was childlike; their impetuosity was in marked contrast to the stolid advance of us Britishers. We were perfectly content to be hemmed in by trench-walls; but not so the Frenchmen. As each turn in the trench was reached, a dozen or more of them would explode with impatience and bound up to the top of the trench, to run across the open country unimpeded on their homeward path.

Our officers had been up to this trench the day before and were thoroughly familiar with it and its contour. Before leaving we had been informed of our individual duties and of the general lay of the land. Hence, on entering this strange trench, we were comparatively at home and quickly settled down into the ordinary routine of trench-life.

The line was quiet at this time. By "quiet" I mean that there was no particular "drive" going on. Of course the Germans have a hatred for absolute quiet, and so, at carefully predetermined occasions, they send over their "coal-boxes" and their "Jack Johnsons," with an occasional *minenwerfer* to punctuate the silence. At hours established in their code of battle they tune up their "Hymn of Hate," but generally this is directed more at the batteries in the rear than at the front line. After weeks of familiarity with the German brand of hate, it becomes nothing more than a method of setting one's watch, so regular is it in its appearance.

One night, shortly after dusk, a despatch-rider wound his way up through the trench and came running to the dugout of the O. C. The arrival of a despatch-rider is not an everyday occurrence, and his appearance usually forms the basis for a tremendous amount of discussion and conjecture as to the possible contents of his message.

So it was tonight. The O. C. took the envelope from him, read the despatch hastily, and immediately the news spread clown the trench that Italy had entered the war and had already mobilized and taken the field.

This news was received with astonishment by our troops, for you must understand that the man in the trenches knows little that is going on, except within a radius of two or three hundred yards. National politics, international intrigues, and the events of which *you* read, are ancient history before *he* ever hears of them. Oftentimes he will receive papers, but always they are three to six days old, and in these stirring times a three-day-old newspaper is as ancient as the *Book of Exodus*. When boundary lines change overnight, when history is being written with every passing moment, even a "last edition" is likely to be mouldy. Hence it is not to be wondered at that the entrance of Italy into the lists came as a distinct surprise, but none the less a welcome one.

Such an unusual event was reckoned worthy of a fitting celebration. Much discussion ensued as to the proper method of signalling the arrival of so gallant an ally. By a burst of inspiration our commanding officer suggested that the Boches be appraised of their newest enemy through the medium of three rounds of rapid fire and three cheers, followed by an immediate plunge for the nearest dugout on the part of the celebrants.

This suggestion received the unanimous approval of the entire battalion, and forthwith three rounds of lead and three rounds of cheers were sent over with equal enthusiasm and despatch. The idea was accepted as a standard method of celebration throughout the line, and from the far right of the British line on across France and Belgium three mighty cheers rang out as a welcome to Italy.

Such exuberance from British troops was diagnosed by the Germans as a preliminary to an attack, and we had hardly made the dug-outs when the roar of German machine-guns echoed our cheers to the horizon.

Perhaps at this point I might dispel one or two illusions which apparently exist in minds not familiar with life in trenchdom. You hear a great deal about a man being "on" for one hour and "off" for four. "On" means that he is "on watch," while "off" means that he is off watch but on the job. There are no union hours in the front line or behind it. While your mechanics are arguing over the necessity for an eight-hour day; while the I. W. W. are striking and rioting to gain themselves a softer seat or a more comfortable job; while Nihilists and Reds of more attractive name, but equally traitorous desires, are holding long meetings and giving vent to windy speeches, your man in the front line is working twenty-four hours a day, and the only thing that keeps him from working longer is the arrival of another day.

Sleep in the front line is a fictitious quantity. There is no such thing. When there are no rations to be carried, there are bombs to be carried; when there are no bombs required, ammunition for the omnivorous machine-guns is urgently necessary; when the machine-gun has its pantry full, there are sand-bags to be filled or communication trenches to be dug. The man in the front line has neither sleep nor holiday. True, he may drop down in his tracks for an hour or two, but he does not *sleep*. His eyes are closed, he is unconscious, but he does not sleep. Over him always broods the possibility of a Hun invasion. His dreams are riotous; he fights and dies a hundred times during that hour; and he rises only slightly refreshed, only a little more ready to do his "bit," as some of you please to call it.

As you review the incessant duties of the front line, you will understand why it is that night loses its meaning, and day likewise. The stand-to order at 3 a. m. does not inconvenience as it would were you a civilian accustomed to rising at six and retiring at ten. There is no conscious day or night when you are in the front line. Each day is just twenty-four indistinguishable hours of interminable toil. Is it any wonder, therefore, that the soldier returns to his rest-billet to drop down absolutely unconscious, blissfully at peace, to sleep for twelve or sixteen hours at a stretch without so much as moving a muscle?

There are no favourites in the front line. It is turn and turn about. The battalion roster shows a record of each man's duties throughout a period of time, and if a man does not volunteer for any particular task, he is assigned whatever task may arise. A daily chore is the ration fatigue. This means bringing up cheese, biscuits, bread, and the nightly jar of rum, or the big "dixies" smoking with a soup concocted from vegetables, meat, etc. There is also the inevitable and much-dreaded jar of jam.

One ration fatigue in which I engaged stands out very clearly in my mind, since it was my first formal introduction to the German gas attack. Gas attacks today have lost some of their initial horror. We have learned how to deal with them. Today the front line listening-posts are on the lookout for such attacks, and when that greenish horror—as innocent in appearance as any cloud, but as deadly as the fumes of old Vesuvius—appears in the foreground, electric-horns blare out their warning to the front line, and on back and back to ten or fifteen miles behind the trenches.

Braziers are also used along the trenches at a distance of twenty or thirty yards. The upflung current of air from these little fires causes the gas to rise and float on and over, without harming those underneath. But in the early days of which I speak, a gas attack was an unknown quantity. Gas shells were a dreaded horror, and gas masks were the most rudimentary affairs imaginable.

We were returning to the front line with our rations, and had almost reached our goal, when there came the scream of a shell, a blinding flash, and then a deafening explosion but a little way ahead of us. It was fifteen or twenty feet away, I should say. Our column of ration-carriers stopped like a man who has been hit a solar-plexus blow. I saw a few of the fellows up front plunge forward or topple over and sink down, as though their legs had been made of putty. A sweet, apple-cider-like smell wafted its way to my nostrils. At first I did not recognize it and took a deeper breath. Instantly I felt as though a giant hand held my lungs. Gradually these hands tightened, and my muscles contracted. I was not suffocating for want of air, but for want of strength to breathe it.

I flung down my load of biscuits and grabbed my gas mask, made only of a piece of medicated cotton and a veil. But it was too late. This grim chlorine giant who held my lungs merely tightened his grasp, and I bounded to the top of the trench and sped away as fast as my legs and a reeling earth would let me. Over to the dressing-station I went, where the medical officer, between spells of violent coughing and spitting of greenish phlegm, dosed me with a vile liquorice compound that somewhat eased my intense discomfort.

All that night I spent under his care, along with three or four other fellows who had likewise managed to stumble over to the station. Shortly afterward four others were brought in. They were too far gone to travel without aid. These boys brought word that four of the fellows had been put out entirely by shell-shock, while six had been thoroughly gassed and were even now hovering on the brink of death.

After the immediate effects of the slight gassing had worn off, I returned to the front line, but for many days thereafter I was intensely weak, and my eyesight was badly dimmed. As a rude warning against future attacks, we filled bully-beef cans with stones and hung them up and down the trench, where a watch could shake them and announce the approach of any sort of gas attack, be it by shell or cloud.

After our spell of duty in the front line we returned to the rest-billets, where the rumble of cartwheels told us that the post was arriving. The carts were piled mountain high with mailbags such as you use in your country, each marked for a certain platoon. Immediately there was jubilation. The sergeant distributed the parcels and letters, and cares and troubles vanished forthwith. Cakes, candy, cocoa, coffee, cheese, butter, books, magazines, and papers were all forthcoming, and how welcome they were! Some poor chaps, perhaps not such good correspondents as the rest of us, were forgotten by the home folks, they stole off into lonesome corners to take What empty cheer they could from the random bits of cake and candy given them by sympathizing comrades.

Let me beseech you never to send a man in the fighting line a case of jam, or even a jar of jam. Jam and mud are synonymous terms in the minds of fighting men. They are fed up on jam. What they want is some of this ready-prepared cocoa or chocolate to which one need only add hot water. Butter is at a premium. Cheese, likewise, is a luxury. Sweet biscuits, hard enough to stand the rough journey, are rare and welcome delicacies. Helmets, trench mirrors, and similar personal accessories are always received with open arms.

The arrival of any packet from home is an event of importance, so don't forget the boys whom you know, when they are on the firing line. The receipt of a letter means as much to them as a trip to the

AFTER THE DAY'S WORK
A BAGPIPER ENTERTAINING HIS COMRADES
BEHIND THE LINES

theatre does to you. A package full of delicacies well, do you remember what a package from home meant to you when you were away at school? Multiply that keen joy ten-fold, add to it the urgent *need* for all such things, and you will have a vague conception of the good that you are doing when you send one of your boys in khaki a little package bearing the brief but welcome sign, "Made in the U. S. A."

Back in the billet our principal duty was the digging of sundry communication trenches in and about the line. I remember that one night a number of us were engaged in digging through an old German trench and enlarging it so that it might better serve our needs. It was awfully hard work, because the straw-thatched dugouts had partially fallen in and matted down in a mass that was almost shovel-proof. Hence it was no surprise to me when my pick struck and stuck fast in what appeared to be a log. I remember kicking away at it, and finally, after loosening it a trifle, I leaned over to remove the offending timber. Locking my hands firmly around it, I braced my feet, gave a giant pull, and tumbled over flat on my back.

But it was no log in which I had imbedded my pick, neither was it a log that I held in my hand. I had a German's boot, and then some besides. The balance of that German was back there under the thatched straw. The horribleness of it, plus the rotten stench, filled me with an ague, and, together with my comrades, I ran back down the trench, where we met the sergeant. He gruffly inquired the reason for our haste. We directed him to follow his nose to the bend, where the reason for our speed would be self-evident. He did as directed, and shortly returned to order us to another part of the line where this most awful reality of the battlefield would not obtrude itself upon our eyes and nostrils.

Returning to the billet that night, after five hours' steady and fatiguing work, we flung ourselves down, tired to the very marrow of our bones. The billet was quiet, except for the occasional snore of a sleeping fighter. Next to me lay a man who had been eternally and everlastingly bragging of his freedom from "seam-squirrels," as we had come to call the crawlers. This name was due to their great preference for the seams of our kilts. As I lay down I noticed this braggard twitching nervously. The twitch grew into a vast convulsion that shook him from head to foot. Suddenly he sat up, looked about furtively, stared at me, and then, thinking that I slept, he clandestinely removed his outer and upper garments and gave way to a luxurious scratching.

The "seam-squirrels" had caught him at last, and in my intense joy at his discomfort—for he had boasted most gloriously of his freedom from attack—I awakened the balance of the company to view his discomfiture. Their joy equalled mine, but only for a little time. There is something about the sight of a man scratching, and taking a keen satisfaction in it, that is contagious. I had not been watching the object of our mirth for more than two minutes before I felt every "seam-squirrel" on my body. They wriggled, they squirmed, they crawled, and they bit. The itch spread over the entire billet, and for the next half hour the night was given over to a revelry of scratching.

Then back to the line we went, and Nichols and I volunteered for advance listening-post duty. At nine o'clock that night we went out. The advance listening-post at this section of the line was fifty yards from the German trench. From one o'clock until two was my time to watch, and it was during this period that Nichols was supposed to sleep. Along about half-past twelve, however, during his watch, the line to our left became "windy," which is trench parlance for nervous and a trifle frightened.

The "windiness" spread from left to right, until the entire line was in an uproar and the Germans were being severely pelted with small-arm fire. The "windiness"' reached its cold finger out into our listening-post, and when it came my turn to watch, Nichols told me that he was going to stand with me, since he was too excited to rest in the bottom of the trench. So we stood up there together, with our eyes just over the top of the sand-bags.

We had been standing there together, shoulder to shoulder for a scant ten minutes, when Nichols slid along the bank toward me and leaned heavily against me. At first I. thought he had gone to sleep from exhaustion, and I turned around to push him upright once more. As I withdrew the support of my body, Nichols collapsed like a straw-man and rolled down into the muddy bottom of the trench.

Even then I did not realize what had happened. I leaned over and lifted his head in my hands. Just then a star-shell shot high up in the heavens above our little hole in the ground, and I saw why Nichols was "exhausted."

Right in the temple he had it, and down his cheek and upon my hand flowed his blood. I watched it like a man in a stupor, so slowly it oozed out dark and warm. Nichols was going west. He opened his eyes a trifle, the lids fluttered, the star-shell went out, and with it went old friend Nichols. He had been my pal from the battle for Lille until this cold wet night out in the front-line listening-post of Vermelles.

I called softly to him, hoping that perhaps he would arouse, if only long enough to say goodbye. But Nick was gone. I covered him with his waterproof sheet and stood up on the firing-step once more. From half-past one until relief arrived I watched there beside Nichols in the sap-head, with the Teuton army only fifty yards away.

They carried him away on a stretcher, and when I returned I went to our captain and asked for a decent burial for Nick. Next morning six of us took him back on the same stretcher on which they had carried him out from his duty. No casket awaited Nick. Only a rough shroud of sacking and a Union Jack. Back to Vermelles we bore him. There we dug a little grave—God, but it was a shallow one!—and lifted old Nick down into it. We stood about with bowed heads for a little while, and that was the only tribute that poor Nichols had.

Then I hurried away, for I could not bear to see the earth, cold and wet, shovelled over that figure which stood for one of the best friends a man ever had, and one of the truest patriots that ever breathed the breath of London's streets or fought in the battle for democracy.

As I wound my way up through the communication trench to the front line, the sport of war was gone, and I swore a solemn oath to avenge Nichols and to make the bullet that sent him west take its quadrupled toll of Germans.

I immediately volunteered for sniper's service, for which I was fitted by my record as a marksman at the training camp. I was accepted, and entered upon my career as a free-for-all sniper in the ranks of His Majesty the King.

Chapter 6

What Happened at Lille

On receiving my credentials as a sniper, the freedom of our section of the trench was given to me, and the sniper's insignia of crossed rifles was emblazoned on my left coat-sleeve.

Owing to the critical and delicately nervous work of the sniper, he is freed from the irksome round of trench duties that are the lot of common soldiery. The day and the night are his to do with as he pleases. His association with the commanding officer is close, much closer than heretofore. He does not even live in the trench, but back a little ways, where the intense strain of constant and watchful waiting may not wear upon his marksmanship.

I had been a sniper for about one week, and had the layout of our section of the trench and of the opposing lines well in mind, when one afternoon our captain, Mr. MacKenzie, came to me and told me of work definitely cut out for us. Our task was to locate and silence a Boche machine-gun which had been proving its effectiveness throughout the previous week.

That night, soon after darkness fell, ten of us crawled out into no-man's-land until we were within one hundred yards of the German trench. Here we divided into five parties of two each, and each party dug itself into a hole. By two o'clock our work was finished, and the dirt we had dug up was spread about over a wide area, so as not to attract the attention of watchful eyes in the opposing trench. In front of our five little holes we had transplanted some of the dank grass which sometimes springs up in no-man's-land under the influence of heavy rain and hot sunshine.

By two o'clock we had finished and had jumped into our burrows, with a sniper and an observer in each burrow. On my rifle I had a telescopic sight and a silencer, the latter making firing practically inaudible. The telescopic sight is one of the devilish ingenuities of modern warfare. It brings the man at the business end of the gun to within almost reaching distance of you. You can pick out any place upon his body, and between the crossed hairlines on the sight you can almost snip the buttons off his coat, if you so wish.

Between our five holes we had strung a string, so that the one who first located the offending machine-gun could signal its exact location to the others. Beforehand we had agreed upon a definite code, and by sun-up we were well along toward locating the object of our endeavours.

By careful listening, combined with the trained eye of our observers, who were aided by their binoculars, we located our gun in a concrete emplacement to the extreme right of our sector of the trench. The sniping officer gave an order that only the snipers on the right of our line of dugouts were to seek out the men behind the Teuton gun.

This gun was very carefully concealed by an elaborate, concrete structure, carefully draped with moss, leaves, and debris, but in the middle of it was a slot about a foot high and two or three feet long. It was through this slot, at a distance of about five hundred yards, that we were to send our shots. Behind it we could see nothing. We had to trust to the guiding instrument of justice to seek out that machine-gun crew.

I presume that I had fired not more than twelve shots when the *rat-a-tat-tat* which had originally revealed it to us died away, to appear no more that day. Perhaps some of our shots reached their mark. Of course I cannot tell and will never know.

Hardly had the machine-gun been silenced, however, when the usual scream of overhead shells changed their tune, and they began dropping woefully close to us. Perhaps we had been located, or perhaps a German observation-balloon, away off to the left, had picked us up. In any event, we dropped down into our dugouts and disappeared completely from the range of vision, but not before two of our boys on the extreme left had been killed by a well-directed Teuton shell. Aeroplanes, too, had been going overhead, unimpeded by any English machines, and in all probability our position had become the public property of the German gunners.

Throughout the balance of that day our lives were a nightmare of expectation, for we did not know when one of those shells would drop into the narrow confines of our individual dugout, and, believe me, there are much more comfortable bedfellows than the German "Jack Johnson."

At the first opportunity after nightfall we sneaked across and over into our own sap-head again, and returned to the rear. On the way back, as we came to a corner of the road, we stumbled over a prone figure, apparently in a dead stupor. The man was drunk. There was no denying it, for you could whiff the odour of rum for many feet about him. He had been sent back for the usual daily rum-ration, and on the return journey had succumbed to the wholesale temptation on his shoulder. Of course our officer had to report him, and as he was an old offender, he was placed under arrest, subject to a drumhead court-martial.

Army life has many punishments, but one of the most extreme is the first-class field punishment which was meted out to this habitual drunkard. It consists in tying a man, with his hands held high over his head, to a convenient tree, door-post, or artillery wheel for two hours each day—one hour in the morning and one hour in the afternoon. This is what is known as the "spread eagle," and it is usually imposed for a period of seventy-two days, at the end of which time any sane man will hurry back to the straight and narrow path of rectitude.

The attitude of the soldiery toward a man so strung up is one of intense hatred and derision. The trained soldier realizes that his life and the lives of all his fellows depends primarily on strict discipline. A man condemned to first-class field-punishment is generally a violator of discipline, and as such well merits the wrath of his entire regiment.

During this period of our stay the German lines were about six hundred yards away, and the soil—typical of all soil in this sector—was chalky. During the hot days of summer the heat radiated from the ground as though it were a hot stove-lid, and this made it doubly difficult to do any accurate firing, owing to mirage. It therefore became our daily duty to fire "test shots" from various listening-posts—shots directed at each foot and each yard of the opposing trenches—in order to keep our marksmanship up to the minute and to accustom ourselves to the annoying mirage that is prevalent during the summer.

Foot by foot we would sweep down the German line, our observers meanwhile watching carefully for the splash of chalk-like smoke that indicated a hit. The necessary corrections, range, and adjustment would be marked down upon a sheet, and so, after a few days of such experiments, we had our entire sector of six hundred yards thoroughly tabulated.

Then we settled down to await the need for our services.

Our preparations had been none too soon, for a German sniper was reported to be giving trouble. He had already hit six of our officers, and his depredations continued unabated.

This German sniper was one of the daredevil variety. I suspect that he must have been a circus clown or a loop-the-loop rider before his entrance into military life. Instead of hiding himself, as is the sniper's custom, this chap would carelessly arise on the parapet, sometimes with a preliminary yell to attract our attention, and then would fire his rifle with exasperating abandon. We came to know him as "Jack-in-the-Box." He would bob up at odd intervals in different sections of the trench. In the morning he might be on the extreme right, in the afternoon on the extreme left, and toward evening in the centre. His very daring seemed to be in his favour, because for over a week we worked on him without success. In the meantime he had accounted for four more of our men. He made a specialty of officers, though, as became one of his daring.

Our corps of snipers quickly fell into bad repute. We dared not enter a trench, unless we cared to take a verbal "strafing" that had the sting of truth behind it. Day after day we waited for him, but always fruitlessly.

One night we snipers got together and agreed upon a definite plan of campaign to wipe out this annoying fellow—and with him the unsavoury reputation that had fallen upon our heads.

The following morning the ten of us set out—each taking as his own a prearranged section of the German trench. We watched all that day, meanwhile revising our ranges and firing adjustments until I personally felt confident that I could split a match, should it be lifted above the Teuton parapet. During our preparations, our friend across the way kept remarkably silent, and we prayed soulfully to ourselves that some random bullet had reached its mark.

But no. On the second afternoon, on the extreme right of the line, we heard the familiar crack of a German rifle. A German rifle makes a different noise than does the English Lee-Enfield. The English gun sounds like the bang of a door, whereas the German rifle makes a noise like the crack of a giant whip—sharp, stinging, and baleful.

Word was passed down the line that "Jack-in-the-Box" was up to his old tricks. He had bagged another officer, and a snarl of derision slipped down the trench to me at the extreme left. As the minutes passed, our German daredevil, as per his usual custom, paraded down his sector of the line and at odd intervals jumped up to taunt us or to fling a shot across. Closer and closer he came to my end of the line.

Just opposite to me was a slight bend in the German trench. I figured that the Teuton sniper would appear here, as it brought him a trifle closer to our line and gave him an opportunity to practise his pet trick of enfilade, or cross-fire. With the assistance of my observer I sought out every foot of this parapet with my experimental shots. I next adjusted my elevation so that future shots would clear the parapet by a scant six inches. Then I waited.

It was a remarkably fine day for sniping. The air was as clear as a bell and there was little mirage to annoy one. Far up to the right I saw the fellow bob up and down, and I figured that my section of the line would be his next appearance. At a word from my observer, I peered through my sight and saw the top of his head moving along the chosen sector of the German parapet. He was playing into my hands for a surety. Evidently, from the motion of his head, he was conversing with someone just below, but hardly enough of his anatomy showed itself as yet to warrant my risking a shot. I had him well covered, and in the powerful telescopic sight I could almost see every hair on his head, for, with typical bravado, he had not bothered to protect himself with the usual gray-coloured cap of a Hun sniper.

Gradually, across the hair-line of my sight, his face appeared, and then his chest. He rested his rifle with his usual debonair flourish, sighted it very carefully, and then apparently the dandy's collar hurt him, for he made a motion as though to stretch his neck and release his Adam's apple from uncomfortable pressure. Through my rifle-sight the whole action was as clear as though it were ten feet away, and I smiled quietly as I pulled the trigger.

There was a crack, my observer shouted, and I could see our friend, the Boche jack-in-the-box, flop forward across the Teuton parapet like a beheaded chicken. The honour of the snipers' corps had been retrieved, and my old friend Nichols had been avenged.

Within a week we moved out of Vermelles to within about five kilometres of Bethune. Our billets were in a wee bit of a village, which for some reason the Germans had marked for shellfire. Throughout our stay there we were under constant punishment, and the business of dodging shells became an obsession with us. I remember that this town, despite its popularity with the German artillery, boasted six untouched *estaminets*. I was in one of them one afternoon when the steady screeching of the shells overhead turned to a more livid scream, and we knew that they were coming our way.

Two blocks away we heard one. Then came an explosion outside that stopped our hearts and pulled the breath out of our lungs. We counted heads, and the twelve of us were still drinking our chocolate unharmed. But not so next door. The shell had fallen in the backyard of the adjoining house, and debris and splinters, flying through the windows, had laid low two of our company. By some stroke of misfortune the two who had gone west through the ministrations of this random shell, directed far behind the line, had been with us unharmed since the very beginning. The Battle of the Marne and the horrors before Lille had left them unscathed. Such is the luck of warfare.

From here we moved back to Bethune, where report had it that a spy was located. Through some means he had been directing the Teuton artillery-fire with uncanny accuracy.

The first morning that I was down in the business district near the railroad yard, I and my comrades noticed what others had already noticed, namely, an unholy number of locomotive-whistles coming from the switching-yard behind the depot. We also noticed that several minutes after each whistle-blast a German shell came over and sought out some particularly vulnerable spot, such as a cross-roads or a warehouse.

We were not the only ones who marked this strange coincidence, and immediately a watch was set upon the railroad yard. Persistent search among the puffing locomotives betrayed the fact that a certain engineer was doing far more than his share of whistle-tooting. Once suspicions were aroused, it was easy to imagine that its toots ran perilously near a code. Furthermore, regardless of where the shells hit, this locomotive seemed always to be at a distant place. In war-time a little suspicion is ample and sufficient ground for action. One does not have to blow up an ammunition-depot in order to be called before a court-martial as a spy. The engineer of the suspected locomotive was taken into custody and subjected to the "third degree," which is about ten degrees hotter than the "third degree" of a police department.

After sufficient persuasion this engineer, who, by the way, was a Frenchman, admitted that he had been working under the orders of a certain alderman or other dignitary of Bethune, who likewise was a Frenchman. He admitted that his whistles had been arranged according to a predetermined code, this code being changed each day.

A daily change of code meant a daily and close communication with the German lines. The means of communication adopted by this traitorous Frenchman was far closer than you might imagine. He had a private telegraph-wire running underground to German headquarters. Over this he had been conversing for some time in a most leisurely and carefree manner.

We need not go into detail as to what happened to these two "patriots." It is sufficient to say that they will not bother Bethune again. I tell this incident as an indication of the fact that German intrigue does not stop with your lowly peasant working in the fields of Flanders, but aspires to higher offices and more noble heads.

At this point in my career one incident stands out with vivid clearness. This was our first bath since coming to the firing-line. Outwardly we were as clean and polished as any diplomat, for such are the rules and regulations of the British army. They say that if you peel away but a generation from a Goorkha, you will have the original stone-age man. I will stand sponsor for the statement that if you peel away the clothing of a soldier who has been in the trenches for six weeks, you will find ample proof of the old adage that *all is not gold that glitters.* Your Tommy's face will shine like Shakespeare's schoolboy; above the collar he will be as scrupulously clean as the kitchen floor of a Holland *hausfrau*; but below that collar's dead-line—or shall I call it dirt-line?—the description can best be left unsung. What you do not know cannot hurt you.

You can imagine that a bath was something of an event. It stands out much more clearly in my mind than does many a trench raid. We bathed in groups of one battalion every few minutes.

There was none of your lazy Sunday-morning bathing. We entered a long room where twenty-five or thirty showers, each in a little private stall, were spouting steam and profanity. At a whistle from the end of the room the showers cast forth twenty-five or thirty fairly presentable Tommies, and another twenty-five or thirty men took their places. The contrast in colour between those entering and those leaving was marked.

Three minutes was the time allowed for bathing. The water started off hot. After about a minute and a half it cooled. When it became cold you knew you had about fifteen seconds remaining for your ablutions.

Three minutes is mighty scant time in which to remove the accumulated filth of weeks. Constant practice in the art of bathing by order did not enable me to complete my toilet in the proper manner. I always had to finish it in the drying room, where we were handed a towel which also performed the offices of a scrub brush.

By this time in its military career our regiment had saddled itself with a reputation. We had been particularly successful in many minor undertakings, and had become known as good men to call upon when something had to be done and done quickly. Our officers invariably volunteered for all sorts of unwelcome duties, and while we gloried somewhat in our reputation, we likewise found it very irksome. Hence it was not with great joy that we received the call to build a road.

Over in your country I believe they sometimes use convicts to build roads. Certainly no self-respecting labouring man would stoop so low. But when you are in the army you do what you are told and consider yourself amply rewarded if you come out alive. Mere fatigue is nothing more than an everyday occurrence. Hence the building of a road called forth little more than the ordinary amount of grumbling.

Four hundred of us went out, armed with picks and shovels, and started digging about three kilometres outside of Bethune, in order to enable the military trucks to avoid the town and the detour and shell-fire that it meant.

We had hardly set to work when a German aeroplane appeared away off in the distance—about five kilometres, I should say. It was headed in our direction. When about three kilometres away, it circled up to about three thousand feet and then swung in a wide ring above our heads. Three men were set to watch it, for even in those days German aeroplanes were not the most welcome visitors to an unarmed body of soldiers.

Report of its arrival was flashed to our aerial squadron, and two of our doughty fighters were sent up to meet it. The German saw them coming and bored straight down upon them. Faintly we could hear his machine-gun ripping out its song. He missed and shot upward again. Our two planes followed suit, and the battle drifted away into the distance, where the nationality of the planes was lost. But we could still see them gyrating like crazy bugs before an arc-light. Up and down, back and forth, they went. At times a head-on collision seemed imminent. But at last our Teuton friend volplaned downward in a long arc that marked him as either hit or fleeing with all speed toward friendly quarters.

Returning to town, we passed a house which had already become familiar to me as the home of Therese. Therese was a French girl who was living with relatives in Bethune. Her former home had been in

88

Lille, and she had been there during the time of the German occupation. I had come to know her very well, and had often called there to pass the time of day and to enjoy some of her family's cooking and good cheer. In fact, I had been taken in as almost a member of the family, and, though my French was extremely weak and their English even weaker, we got on in jolly good fashion.

As I passed that evening, she and her relatives were sitting out in front of their house enjoying the cool of coming night, so I called out a rather broken invitation to take a walk. To this she heartily assented. It was during this walk that she told me some of her first-hand experiences during the German occupation of Lille.

It seems that Therese had been living with her aged grandparents, her father and mother, and a younger brother and sister. The Germans' first move, on entering Lille, had been to ransack the entire town. Her grandfather, an old warrior and a fighter still, despite his years, had come upon one of his friends being brutally beaten by a German officer in the street. Therese told me that her grandfather was not familiar with the German order concerning firearms, and had immediately rushed into his home and taken a pot-shot at the officer from the window. The sound of the shot brought a horde of Germans from all directions, and the entire household was hauled into the street for "examination," as the officer in charge was pleased to call it.

This "examination" consisted of brutally maltreating the womenfolk and lining the menfolk of the household up before them for immediate despatch by a firing-squad. The latter was made up of practically the entire company of Germans, all of whom appeared insanely anxious to prove their marksmanship at twenty yards.

The women were then brought to headquarters. Therese's mother and grandmother were sent in opposite directions, and Therese was detained. Fortunately she had not been put under heavy guard, and had been able to procure a peasant boy's outfit of clothing. This she donned and, travelling by night, managed to pierce the German lines and to reach our own lines in safety, as an itinerant peddler.

This much Therese told me of her own experiences. She said little of the actions of the Germans toward herself, though from that little one could gather much. The Teutons had ransacked every home in Lille, and of those who stayed, many were shot for imaginary or entirely fictitious causes. Everything in the city had been carried away. Pictures fastened to the walls were slashed so as to utterly destroy their value. Every bit of iron, steel, copper, and lead had disappeared. All families had been utterly separated. The men had been sent away in one direction and the women in another.

I say that the women were sent away. The women were not *all* sent away. As fast as the Germans could operate, the men of Lille were taken to one end of the town and all the women to the other. Here the younger women were separated from the older, and the older women were sent away to goodness knows where. The younger women were taken before the commanding officer. I need not carry the story further. Enough has already been written about German methods. Let me merely add that little bits which I pieced together from Therese's story added a mighty weight to all that now rings in our ears as samples of German *kultur*.

In speaking of the Germans' treatment of the womenfolk, Therese seldom spoke of the private German soldier. It was usually the officers. In recording this, however, I do not feel that I hang any laurels on the virtue of the Teuton private. He never had a chance at the womenfolk. German orders are, "officers first."

Before the war I have heard of the unspeakable boorishness of the German officer. I know enough of the German officer's attitude toward womenfolk in peace-time to imagine what his attitude would be toward hostile, defenceless women in war-time. But my imagination has proven a weak and effeminate thing. Therese's tale of German tortures, reinforced by other and equally authoritative tales that I heard, allows me to know beyond peradventure of a doubt that the German creed today, (as at time of first publication), reads, "Kill, but enjoy even as you kill."

That evening reinforced our friendship, and her recitation of the troubles she had undergone brought Therese closer to me. We agreed to exchange lessons in French and English. These had progressed only a little way, however, when we were again ordered away, and, as a parting jest, I asked her to write to my mother, saying that I did not have the opportunity to write her before leaving. Therese took my jest in earnest, however, and my mother treasures today a four-page letter from this little French girl who had been through the horrors of Lille, but still had heart enough to write a British Tommy's mother that he was well and happy, and, like all the English, was doing "his bit."

There is one phase of "doing your bit" of which you hear but little. That is the "Blue Funk," or "Firing Squad." In the armies of your labouring men the man who does not do his earnest best is discharged. The man who disobeys orders is subject to nothing worse than a reprimand. But "over there," as you please to call it, we get no reprimand, and the man who does not do his earnest best meets nothing weaker than a court-martial.

Our own regiment never found it necessary to have a "Blue Funk Squad." Plainly, the duty of such a squad is to execute those guilty of insubordination or cowardice. Cowardice is the commonest of trench troubles. To *feel* cowardice is no crime, but to *show* cowardice is punishable by death. A good friend of mine, an officer, told me that all the firing squads in kingdom come could not have held him in the front line during a heavy shelling. He said that only the fear of losing the respect of his men kept him with them. This statement from an officer who is now decorated for bravery will give you some indication of the fear that very naturally prevails in the front-line trenches during an attack.

Fear of the firing squad, in all probability, keeps few men from showing cowardice. I honestly believe that the honour of the regiment and the fear of what other men will think holds more men to their duty in the face of danger than does any firing squad in Flanders. Oftentimes I will vouch for the fact that a sudden and sure death is far preferable to the hellish waiting. I believe that before Lille some of us would have run back, firing squad or no, had not the honour of the regiment been at stake. It is the honour of the regiment, reinforced by stern discipline, which holds you in your place.

Once more let me emphasize to all American troops the need for rigid obedience to discipline. You may not receive war's real discipline while training in America, or even while training in France, but when you get up into the front line *discipline must be observed*.

It is one of the million things which will win the war for democracy. It is so rigidly inforced among English troops that a man who does not return on time from leave in London is shot after only a very formal court-martial. Cowardice gives no opportunity to plead an alibi. Lateness from leave permits you to plead extenuating circumstances. But believe me, my friend, little short of drugging or a blackjack on the head in a dark alley will prove sufficient alibi for a stern military court-martial.

Therefore I say, respect your officers, respect them not only as *men*, but as the representatives of that central and unifying intelligence by which alone this war will be won.

CHAPTER 7

The Spy at Headquarters

From Bethune we were again sent up to the firing-line twelve kilometres distant. On the way, as we neared the front, we encountered dugouts filled with reserve soldiery. This was a new system recently adopted by the British, and displaced the old method of quartering reserves far behind the line. It made them more mobile and enabled a given sector to be handled by fewer troops.

No sooner had we reached the front-line trench than word was passed to us to be on the lookout for a German machine-gun emplacement which had been so carefully hidden by the Germans that it had clicked its toll of death for over ten days without being located.

It fell to the lot of McKenzie and myself that evening to stand watch at a listening-post about fifty yards from the German front line. It was a peculiarly nasty evening; a fine rain pelted down, and a cold breeze that belonged more in March than in June chilled one to the marrow. Hardly had we taken our places when word reached us that a bombing-party of Germans might be expected at any moment. This same bombing-party had made itself thoroughly obnoxious for three nights running, and it was to be expected that it would continue its depredations until interrupted by the sudden demise of its members.

With this reassuring news to cheer us on, we took our places on the fire-step. At eleven o'clock I went on duty. As is the custom, I came off duty one hour later and stretched myself out at the bottom of the dugout, while McKenzie stood watch.

At 12:30 a sergeant came running out to the sap-head. He asked us if we had heard any suspicious noises. Upon receiving a negative reply, he explained that our machine-gun emplacement, which commanded a neighbouring road, had been entirely wiped out by the German bombing-party but three minutes before. Hardly were the words out of his mouth when our entire line burst forth into a blaze of flares and musketry, and, clearly outlined in the middle of no-man's-land, we could see the German party scurrying across, like rats in an open field.

Immediately an enfilading fire from our machine-guns reached out for them. It wavered for a moment to their right, and then it swept across them, clung to them, and another German bombing-party was wiped out.

But still the obnoxious Teuton machine-gun emplacement remained a mystery, and it became the duty of six of us, under the command of an officer, to go out the following evening and put a quietus upon this obstreperous gun.

We went about ten o'clock, armed only with trench-knives and revolvers. Between us was stretched a rope, much after the fashion of Alpine climbers. The usual code of signals had been arranged so that the lieutenant in front could inform any or all of us of his intentions. It was our little job to locate the exact position of the machine-gun emplacement. It had already been partially located, but to make doubly sure we were to send up a flare at the precise point in the German line where this machine-gun held forth.

It is a comparatively simple and safe matter, barring accidents, to merely investigate the opposing front line, but to send up a flare within a few yards of the opposing line is to beard the lion in his den. Yet this was part and parcel of our duty, and we went at it morally certain that few, if any, of us would return to our own lines. Three of the boys had bombs, and before leaving we all wrote letters home and made our last will and testament. These we left in charge of our comrades, for it looked like certain death.

Out to the nearest sap-head we went. This was about six hundred yards from our approximate objective. With final instructions to the men in the sap-head, we set out. No-man's-land at this point was as bare as the top of a billiard-table, except here and there where a shell-hole punctuated the landscape or a bit of stubble remained, cut down close to the ground by the machine-gun-fire of the opposing lines.

What few flares there were gave but little light, owing to the high wind and the misty, driving rain. Half way across there came a tremendous tug at the rope, and we all fell flat on our faces. Not twenty yards away, against the horizon, we could see the outlines of a German working-party. It was investigating our lines, repairing barbed wire, or doing some other duty of a sort peculiar to no-man's-land.

ADVANCING IN SKIRMISH ORDER AGAINST THE ENEMY

Flat on our faces we remained for the better part of ten minutes, until it was accurately determined that the German working-party had retired to its own trenches. Then, with infinite pains, we worked our way up, half-crawling, half-standing, to the very front of the German barbed wire. We could hear the Teutons talking and laughing, but the outlines of their machine-gun emplacement remained hidden.

Up and down in front of the Teuton line we crawled, watching for any break in the parapet or any change of colouring which might disclose the object of our search. At last three jerks from our officer brought us to attention, and in response to his code directions we dimly discerned the vague outlines of an emplacement, carefully hidden by debris and withered stubble.

According to previously arranged plans, our bombers took up a position about ten yards to the right and left of the emplacement. Our officer then gave a signal, and our flare shot up into the night but a scant fifteen yards from the German front-line trench.

You may wonder why it was necessary to set off the flare so close to the Hun stronghold. It was only by so doing that the lookouts in our sap-head could obtain the angle of fire necessary to reach the suspected machine-gun. Had we gone back and depended only upon our sense of direction for the location of this emplacement, it would have remained a mystery indefinitely. But by drawing a sight from the listening-post on the right and left, we were enabled to accurately mark its position and to wipe it out on the following day.

But to return to the moment in which the flare hissed its way up through the driving rain. It had hardly left the revolver of the officer in charge, when the bombers hurled their charges full into the German trench and the whole line, both Teuton and British, sprang to its feet in an ecstasy of nerves. No-man's-land swam in a ghostly, yellow light. Machine-guns on both sides began to sing their lay, and over a thousand yards along the front a miniature battle immediately sprang into being.

It was through this cross-fire that we of the observation party were expected to make our return. By taking advantage of every scratch and shell-hole upon the surface of the ground, five of the six of us managed to drag ourselves back to our sap-head. Only one remained out in no-man's-land, and the next morning we saw him there, still close to the Teuton front line.

During this period of my duty on the front line there was little, if any, heavy firing, but considerable scout-work was necessary as a preliminary to an offensive at a somewhat later date. The location of the above German machine-gun emplacement was but a small part of the work in the preparation for a big attack. Before any attack of importance is undertaken it is necessary to know the opposing line as well as the Teuton himself does. Each machine-gun, each field-piece, each trench-mortar and even each sap-head must be carefully plotted and marked.

One of the many strategic points of this sector was an old farmhouse lying midway between the German and the British line. The opposing trenches were approximately eight hundred yards apart, and between them, a mere wreck, stood this old shambles of a house. One hundred and fifty yards from its doorway, in the direction of our trenches, stood a pump. Here we had been accustomed to obtain some of the most delicious well-water that I have ever tasted, and it had become one of the duties of the ration-party to secure a liberal quantity from this well, even though it was done at a considerable risk to themselves.

The Germans, however, early discovered our fondness for the well, and it was not long before they had thoroughly poisoned it and spoiled it for several generations to come. Not content with this, however, they had a way of sneaking into the farmhouse with snipers and a portable machine-gun, and from this point would direct a nasty fire up and down our sector of the line.

Occasionally we would return the compliment, but as we knew nothing of the casualties caused by our own snipers and knew only what the Germans had done to us from the same location, it was determined that the next German party to take possession of this house would get its just deserts.

We had not long to wait. That very evening, just at dusk, the song of a German machine-gun piped out from the second-story window of the house. A call went back to our artillery to bestow a few pieces of high explosive in the general direction of the farmhouse. But the reply was that they had no ammunition to waste on such small trifles. This was early in the war, when the Germans were easily throwing two shells to our one, and even at that we were carefully husbanding our scant supply.

Since the artillery refused to aid us, it became our pleasure to do the job alone. Twelve of us volunteered for this service. I was one of the twelve. We waited until dark, and then set out across the four hundred yards that separated us from the house.

In the meantime the Germans had been extremely quiet, and we began to suspect that they had escaped us. But they were only biding their time.

As we reached the well they evidently sighted us, or sighted a suspicious movement, and the machine-gun spat at us from its usual window just above the doorway. There was nothing to do but fall flat and scuttle up to the house as best we could. When we came within fifty yards there was no mistaking the fact that the Germans had spotted us. Both the machine-gun and the snipers were doing their best to beat us in our race for the house. Our officer shouted out the command: "Six to the back; and six to the front!" I happened to be one of the six who went to the front.

We found the door barricaded, and above us was the machine-gun and four very accurate and skilful snipers. One by one the boys about me slipped down to their knees, victims of the fire from the upper window. I emptied the chambers of my revolver without any apparent effect, and then found myself alone, sheltered only by the scanty protection of the portal of the door. I silently thanked a hard-working ancestry who had made me as thin as the proverbial rail. A fat man would have found my position about as much protection as a dollar umbrella.

Here I stood for a minute or two, with five of my comrades at my feet. Every one of them had been victims of the snipers' bullets. Then I heard the racket of the party that had gone to the rear. Trusting to sheer luck and to the fact that the same noise would be heard by the Germans, who would then be drawn from the window, I made a run for it. Thus I managed to get around the corner of the house without attracting the Teuton fire.

At the back I found the boys just breaking into the house. Up the stairs the seven of us rushed as one man. The Germans were barricading the door of the room, but the scanty furniture that remained in the house afforded little material for their purpose. Presently we burst into their quarters, after only trifling work with an old chair which served us as an improvised, but effective, battering-ram.

Instead of being greeted by a volley of shots, as we had expected, we found five Germans on their knees, with hands uplifted, and the words *"Kamerad! Kamerad! Mercy!"* spouting from their lips like some well-rehearsed chorus.

It was the same old piffle that you hear from every German when you have him cornered, and it met with a cold reception at our hands.

Our officer took the floor and replied:

"Little enough mercy you showed us a few weeks ago down by Lille! You had plenty of time to cry for mercy when we were coming across that last five yards. When mercy is yours to give, you never give it. You cut my pal's throat like some porker; you blinded our lieutenant! Mercy? Hell!"

With that the bayonets in our hands got busy, and there were five less Germans to wear the Iron Cross that night.

I do not believe I am telling anything amiss when I say that since the battle for Lille we Scottish have taken few, if any, prisoners. You will remember how the Black Watch went over the top and at the German trenches. You will remember how some thirty of them reached the Teuton lines, and how they returned, stripped of all accoutrements, to be shot down like rats. With such a picture ever before us, do you wonder that the Scottish do not find it in their hearts to take German prisoners? Do you blame us men, who saw in those five Germans an opportunity to demonstrate that *kultur* can work both ways? There are those who prate loudly of turning the other cheek. I suspect, however, that these same pacifists, were the Germans entrenched at Schenectady or Buffalo, would find scant chance to turn the other cheek. Give a German an inch, and he will take a mile. The only cure for the German atrocity is to fight fire with fire. The man who can see his own pal and comrade shot down in cold blood, as we had seen the Germans shoot down our Black Watch, is not a man, if he can refrain and hold back his hand from avenging such slaughter.

From this work we went back to Vermelles again, to our rest-billets. Vermelles at this time was known to the Germans as one of our main arteries, and hence it was subject to a constant shelling which waxed intense at specified hours of the day.

Running along beside our billet was an old trench which had seen service in the early days. It ran almost without interruption to the very door of an *estaminet* about half a mile distant. This trench afforded ideal protection to the hungry soldier, except for a scant one hundred and fifty yards of its length, where it crossed a meadow and became merely a hollow depression in the surface of the ground. The Germans had this spot carefully marked and sighted, and to cross it was to flirt with death with a vengeance. Nevertheless the lure of the estaminet drew our whole company across this one hundred and fifty yards once or twice or even three times a day, when opportunity and the O.C. permitted. Of course the practice was frowned upon, although no formal order had been given forbidding us to go.

One afternoon, while off duty, with some dozen or more of my fellows I broke the unwritten law and made a dash across the open ground without fatalities. Reaching the estaminet in safety, we sat down on its little porch. We were sipping our grenadine when the usual German "strafing" of Vermelles began.

The bombardment of a town is one of the most spectacular sights. It is beautiful in a terrible way, if observed from a generous distance. From our refuge we could watch it without fear of becoming active participants in the destruction.

You would hear a German gun boom, there would be a scream overhead, and then, after a pause, a terrific explosion, just close enough to make it interesting and to observe the effect accurately. As each shell hit—the Germans were using high explosives liberally that day—a geyser of dirt and red brick-dust shot up into the air, like some tremendous oil-gusher. So violent was the shelling that afternoon that the entire town of Vermelles seemed covered by a haze of black and red. Interspersed with the fumes and dust, occasional little cotton-puffs of shrapnel appeared. At intervals a house would slide out of sight, the victim of concussion. Through binoculars we could see whole dwellings lifted into the air, as if they had been toys, to be cast down as mere piles of smoking ruins.

The German shelling lasted for about an hour without drawing fire from our artillery. At its conclusion, however, our observation balloon, in conjunction with our aeroplanes, had located and sighted a German brewery considerably behind their lines. In the cupola of this brewery the Teutons had installed a machine-gun which had been traversing up and down our lines for two or three days.

No sooner did we sight this brewery than an urgent plea went forth to our artillery to direct their efforts upon it, and particularly upon the waspish occupant of the cupola. Word came back that they could afford but five shells. An aeroplane went up to check the observation and to make doubly sure of the accuracy of our aim. The first shell fell short, the second crept up just a trifle, and the third hit the cupola about ten feet below its base and exploded. Cupola, Germans, and machine-gun jumped into the air, an indiscriminate mass of dust and smoke.

To incapacitate a German machine-gun is an insult; to incapacitate a German machine-gun in a brewery is a triple insult. Immediately the wrath of the Germans was reawakened, and for two hours Vermelles and all the intervening territory bore up under a tremendous shelling from practically every field-gun on the Teuton front. Our own guns were silent, of necessity, a necessity created partly from fear of being located and partly because of their scant supply of ammunition.

And right here let me put in a plea for ammunition.

You workers in the shops and factories, how little do you realize the intense need of the front line! We boys out here work, yes, we slave, for twenty-four hours a day, Sundays and holidays, rain or shine. You in your comfortable homes, with all the conveniences and luxuries of modern city life, just remember us out here and give us all you've got.

The man who stays at home to make shells or to make any of the munitions of war, or, for that matter, any of the tools which go to make these munitions, is not a "slacker." We need him; we need hundreds and thousands of him. But the man who stays at home to make munitions and then takes every opportunity to lay off or to cut his time is a "slacker." He is worse than a "slacker," for not only does he keep from us the fruits of his own efforts, but he keeps from us the fruits of another man's efforts, a man who might give us all he had.

When we are up on the front line and read newspaper accounts of munition-workers striking or complaining, it brings a smile, a wry smile, to our lips. We can't help comparing your position with ours. We can't help thinking of the few cents per day that we receive for giving everything we've got, including our lives, perhaps. We can 't help comparing our offering with the security, the peace, and the comfort which you receive in return for your skill and handicraft. If every munition-worker, if every worker on tools or accessories that go to make up munitions could only spend a short half-hour in a front-line trench, there would be little cause for the cry that echoes back from Flanders:

"Send us shells, and shells, and more shells!"

I remember hearing the story of a visit of munition-workers to the front-line trench. It will tend to prove my statement.

Word was passed up the line that a deputation from the English Munition-Workers was coming to see if we *actually* needed more shells. Those boys back home evidently didn't care to take our word for it. They knew that they were making hundreds, yes, thousands, of shells every day, and it probably appeared to them as the height of waste that we could use them all and still be demanding more.

When word reached us that their committee was about to visit us, a gurgle of anticipation ran down the trench, for here indeed was an opportunity to demonstrate the horrors of war to those most in need of a demonstration.

Our officer, although he said little, managed to egg us on in our plans for deviltry, and he went back to meet the deputation of munition-workers with a sardonic smile on his face.

They stepped out of a staff automobile, wearing Prince Albert coats and tall silk hats. Unquestionably they were a stunning spectacle, a striking contrast, incidentally, to the grim khaki uniform seen everywhere along the front.

Our commanding officer, instead of leading them through the usual communication-trenches, which were only about ankle-deep in mud, chose to lead them through a main drain-trench. A main drain-trench is somewhat similar to an intercepting sewer. It is designed to carry off the mud and water from some several hundred yards of trench. This particular drain-trench happened to be waist-deep in slimy silt. Three feet of this obnoxious mud was the introduction of our diplomats from London to the horrors and inconve iences of war.

When word reached us that they were in our midst, our artillery, rising to the occasion, sent a salvo of fire over into the German lines. Never before had this failed to bring back a triple dose of German steel, but today, for some unaccountable reason, no such reply came. The artillery tried its luck once more, and spent a dozen more of its precious shells, but still no reply came back.

The quiet became embarrassing. Not a machine-gun spoke; not a sniper's rifle cracked across at us. Something had to be done, for the situation was growing desperate.

A non-commissioned officer had an inspiration,—or perhaps it had all been planned beforehand. In any event, dugouts were ransacked and every available bomb was prepared for action. As the munition-workers slowly ploughed their way down the drain-trench, every one took an armful of bombs and, with rifles pointed in air and machine- guns directed anywhere, began a little battle of their own, a "personally conducted" battle, so to speak.

Never was there a more realistic duplication of the front line when a big drive is on.

Bear in mind that the munition-workers were waist-deep in mud. Their progress was slow, and they were hidden from our front line and our little comedy by a parapet.

For about thirty minutes our boys staged one of the most complete and harmless battles of the war. As no word came to desist, it became apparent that their efforts were meeting with the appreciation of the commanding officer. They redoubled them. Blood-curdling yells and shrieks combined with the noise and smoke of exploding grenades, until hell itself seemed to have been turned loose in this particular sector of the trench.

All the time the Germans had been serenely quiet, although a demonstration such as this on any other day would have called forth the severest reprimand in the shape of a bombardment of an hour or more.

To our left at this time was a bridge, known among the boys as "London Bridge." It spanned a little stream which ran across no-man's-land between the German and English lines. No one, to date, had been able to cross this bridge alive, and you can imagine our astonishment when we saw our officer lead the deputation of munition-workers to the bridge-head and invite them to cross.

This seemed to be carrying the farce a little too far, but the officer evidently knew his business, for very graciously and politely he invited them to cross *first*, saying that he would follow them.

To our horror, they started across, graphic illustrations of the old adage that *"ignorance is bliss."* We fully expected to see them wiped out before they had gone ten feet, but not only did they go ten feet, but half way across, and then loitered on the edge and viewed the scenery thereabouts.

Not a shell or rifle-shot came over from the German lines. They were as quiet as a tomb. After a brief conference in the centre of the bridge, the bedraggled, mud-soaked deputation moved on, followed by our commanding officer on the run. He had hardly made the crossing when a German high-explosive shell screamed after him. By sheer luck it alighted only a hundred yards from the munition-workers. Three of our boys gave up their lives to this shell, but never have lives been given to better advantage. The munition-workers were tremendously impressed. They told our commanding officer that they had long desired to see a tremendous battle, and now that they had seen one and had tasted the horrors of war, they were going to return and do their utmost to double and triple Britain's output of shells. They also announced that, as they had a tremendous amount to do that day, they would like to hurry away. Back they went, firmly convinced that the front line does need "shells, and shells, and more shells."

You may wonder why the Teutons were so quiet. We wondered,

too, until a few days later a German spy, serving in the capacity of interpreter at our headquarters, was captured and given the usual punishment meted out to such gentry. The coming of these ammunition-workers had been common talk about headquarters for days, and their contemplated arrival had been duly forwarded to the Germans. With their usual cleverness, the latter had forecast the result of absolute quiet, and so withheld their fire in the hope that the munition-workers would be influenced and that as a result our supply of shells would diminish, rather than increase.

It may interest you to know that this same spy had been intimately connected with the failure of our attack at Lille. He was the man who warned the Germans of the impending assault. I have since heard prisoners say that the Germans expected us three days before we struck. They admitted this very frankly, when captured. As a matter of fact, the battle for Lille *was* planned for a Thursday. You will remember that it didn't take place until the following Sunday. It had been postponed at the last minute.

This same spy had also been connected with our cordial hostess who had the friendly pup who wore a hollow collar. It was through the medium of this dog that he forwarded despatches to the German lines, and it was by his efforts that they were advised of the old lady's arrest. With his arrest and confession many peculiar "coincidents" were cleared up and vanquished for all time.

While returning from watching the bombardment of Vermelles I inadvertently allowed myself to be observed by a German sausage-balloon, or by some company of snipers, and became the recipient of a cordial dose of shrapnel and musketry fire. I needed no second invitation to hasten my pace, and bounded around the corner of my billet, only to run head-on into my officer. He spun round like a top, and fell on the back of his neck with a resounding thud.

Springing to his feet in a rage, he roundly abused me, first as a ruffian, and then, as sober judgment returned to him, as a man who had disobeyed orders by going down the communication-trench to the *estaminet.* Partly as punishment for disobeying orders, and partly as a handy vent for his spleen, he sentenced me to an extra fatigue. This consisted in carrying wire and other engineering tools up to the front line to repair barbed-wire fences and to aid in similar work.

My duties were to begin immediately. At nightfall, with a company of about fifteen others who were loaded down with tools and accessories of all sorts, I crawled along "Shrine Road," so called because of the little shrine set up at its intersection with the communication-trench. "Shrine Road" ran parallel to the German lines and was often subject to heavy shell- and musketry-fire. It so happened on this evening that the moon was at our back. We must have been neatly outlined to German snipers, for we had hardly set out when the entire surrounding territory jumped up in little puffs of dust, each marking the landing-place of a German bullet.

We immediately took to the ditch and dragged our heavy tools to the communication-trench. But, even so, we were still observed and were subjected to a heavy machine-gun fire, which swept across at a nasty angle and bagged three of the boys.

Our line at this point bent back from the German line in a great half-circle. Thus to command it required practically double the number of men. It was the work of this evening to straighten this bend and so release the men there for service elsewhere.

As soon as darkness fell we went over the top from a listening-post. There were about one hundred and fifty of us on the job. The German lines were about five hundred yards away. Five hundred yards is not a great distance when there is nothing between you and the German fire. But fortunately our occupation was not discovered, and we spread out across no-man's-land in a ragged line and began to scratch ourselves in with the enthusiasm of a bull-pup seeking a long-buried bone.

At frequent intervals we would hear across the stillness of the night the preliminary hiss of a flare, and, from a forest of bobbing heads, no-man's-land became as vacant as a cemetery, to all outward appearances, at least.

We were barely well started on our work, when our outposts' screen, about thirty feet in front of us, reported a strong German working-party coming our way. Rifles were hurriedly secured and loaded, and available protection was at a premium. By good fortune, however, the working-party drifted in the opposite direction, and before the first streaks of dawn crept up over the horizon a neat trench had been prepared. The dirt had been evenly distributed over several yards, so that even from the German observation-balloon our new position was not apparent.

This shortening of the line and all the preliminary work in plotting the machine-guns of the opposing forces was merely the prelude to a local attack. This took place one evening shortly after dusk, when five hundred yards of our line went over the top and at the Bavarians, who

The London Scottish detaching a truck

commanded the Teuton trench at this sector.

The Bavarians have a reputation as veritable fire-eaters. On this occasion they did not live up to their repute. The previous evening our scouts had cut long lanes through the German barbed wire, and, preceded by our bombers, we rushed across no-man's-land without preliminary artillery preparation, depending largely on surprise for success.

The surprise was not total, although it was sufficient for the purpose. We were almost up to the German barbed wire before their lookouts scented our approach. Two minutes later five hundred of us jumped down as one man into their trench. Considering the suddenness of the attack, the Germans were fairly well-prepared. I remember that my leap carried me squarely upon the back of a stalwart Teuton, who jabbed upward at me with his bayonet as I plunged down. The shock of my arrival on his shoulders diverted his aim and likewise scattered us both over several yards of trench. He recovered himself first. With a guttural oath, he drew back his rifle—it looked as big as a telegraph pole—as a preliminary to running me through.

Up to this time I had regarded tales of one's last moments as being largely of a mythological nature. I had heard that in the last few seconds of a man's existence his entire life runs through his brain like a panorama. I now had good cause to repent of my ridicule, for every little detail of my twenty-two summers flashed upon me in intimate retrospect.

The German's gleaming blade, seemingly with infinite slowness, crept down upon me. But it never reached me, thanks to my commanding officer, who was just behind me. There was the crack of a revolver, and the German pitched forward on top of me, his rifle spinning out of his hand and over the top of the trench. My fear-bound muscles relaxed, and I sprang to my feet, recovered my rifle, and rushed for a communication-trench, which by this time was crowded with a milling mass of Teuton and Scottish soldiers.

As I plunged around the corner I ran plump into a six-foot specimen of a Bavarian. He loomed up out of the night like an ox. There is no mistaking these chaps, even in the dark. Their outlines are different, their helmets are shaped differently, and their packs are placed differently. I think my arrival was as much a surprise to him as his arrival was to me. Our rifles, bayonet first, went back over our heads like one, but I was quicker on recovering. I lunged forward, forgetful of all the instructions of our bayonet-tutor back in England. But perhaps I *did* remember them subconsciously, for my bayonet found its mark neatly under the chin of the Bavarian. At the time I felt no special anxiety about his future conduct, for he collapsed with a grunt. I pulled my rifle out—it had been almost jerked from my hand by his weight—and rushed on to assist my comrades in the communication-trench.

By this time the Bavarians were in full retreat back to their second line. Some of our boys in their eagerness had followed them across the open ground above the trench. This was unfortunate, for all of these lost their lives, owing to the fire of our machine-guns which were directed indiscriminately toward the fleeing Germans.

With the winning of the last yard of trench, we each pulled from our belt three sandbags, and the communication-trenches were barricaded and fully covered by enfilading machine-guns. It was only then that we had time to cool off and review the evening's work. Probably the entire attack and the completion of our barricade had not taken more than half an hour at the outside, but, as we sifted back into the trench proper and the heat of battle left us, some of the horror of it took possession of us.

There were Germans all around, and there were some of our boys, too. One group still flashes up before me in the night. It was a German and a Scotty, locked in each other's arms. Each had run the other through with his bayonet at precisely the same instant, and they had closed in death's embrace, to remain there until we pulled them apart.

CHAPTER 8

The British Air Service Becomes Stronger

In the face of the many accounts of aeroplane fights with which we are regaled today, any of the little aeroplane battles which I observed in the beginning of the struggle seem puny and weak. You must remember that in 1915 the aeroplane was in its infancy. Indeed, at that date, even though the Germans had few planes,—they preferred the Zeppelin—their aerial forces generally held dominance over those of the English. Both sides used extensively what planes they had, but the battle-plane was in its cradle, and a single type of plane often served as observation-, scout-, and battle-plane in one. This made the struggle of opposing planes none the less interesting, however, although considerably rarer than today, (as at time of first publication).

At some time in your experience in the front line you are likely to be appointed to aero-scout-duty. In this capacity you are instructed to keep an eagle eye out for any approaching *Taubes* and to sound two shrill blasts on a whistle as an announcement of their approach.

At such times every one had iron-clad orders to seek cover immediately. There must be no delay, the idea being to impress the German observer with the absolute bareness of the landscape and to hide from him any troop movements.

Outside Vermelles I remember seeing one of the prettiest battles between an aeroplane and our anti-aircraft guns that it has ever been my privilege to observe. It was one of those wonderfully clear June days, ideally adapted to aeroplane observation. The sun had just swung up over the horizon, when through my binoculars I caught the approach of a German *Taube*, with its characteristic black cross on the under wing.

I announced the fact to our anti-aircraft gunners, and they immediately wheeled their guns into position, in order to reach the German when he was practically overhead. He swung about in wide, cautious circles for five or ten minutes, and then, at a word from the commander of the anti-aircraft guns, there came the ripping crash, thrice repeated, of a three-barrelled rifle.

Perhaps you have observed a display of fireworks from across a lake or a field. You will remember the sharp crack of the mortars, the long wait, and then the burst of multicoloured stars high up in the heavens, followed by the crackle of distantly exploding rockets. The bombardment of an aeroplane affords much the same spectacular display. There is the sharp *boom—boom—boom* of the anti-aircraft gun, and then the wait while the shells spin their way upward. Presently there are three splashes of cotton, which spray out in jagged lines across the heavens, and from far off comes the ominous crackle of the exploding shrapnel.

We had quite a force of anti-aircraft guns concentrated on the German, and he turned his nose upward in order to escape the deluge. But we got him. The gunner to our left reached up and apparently crippled his engine or punctured his gasoline-tank. In any event, either his engine or his control was badly shattered, for he spun like a top, righted himself, and then staggered first one way and then the other, like a drunken bat.

You could not help admiring the fellow and the skill which he exhibited. In long, inebriated vol-planes he slid down and down, until he was only about a thousand feet above us, when he apparently exerted every effort to obtain control over his staggering craft. But it was of no avail. High above our heads he plunged backward, and then shot down like a comet to the ground.

Of course, since the early days of the war we have heard more or less of atrocities. In your country I have seen and talked with people who hold the opinion that atrocities are a myth. That no war has ever been fought without the occurrence of *some* atrocities is true. A thousand or a million men cannot be gathered together without some of them overstepping commands and decency. But from all corners of the line word kept seeping in to us of peculiarly horrible mutilations practiced by the German troops.

I have heard it said that such atrocities are practiced under orders of the German High Command. I will take no issue with this fact. I have heard the German High Command blamed for all atrocities.

Neither will I argue this point. I only know that the man who *commits* the atrocity is the German *private*. He may be acting under orders, but the blood is on his hands, though the legal blame may reach higher.

I myself place full blame upon the German *trooper*, the private, for the atrocities which I know to have been practiced. Whether he is acting under orders or not does not influence my decision. I only know that if *our* officers—or yours—asked *their* men to practice the brutalities so common among German troops, those officers would either be accidentally (?) shot or openly disobeyed. The only possible alibi I can see for the German trooper's actions and his obedience to orders from higher up is the propaganda which has been pumped into him from earliest childhood. He has been "fed up" on the beauties of lust and blood. He has been taught that God smiles on the German murderer. Any man who is fool enough to believe this sort of slime has no excuse, in my eyes, for his obedience.

There has been considerable talk in your country of exaggeration, of falsification, in reporting German atrocities. Therefore it is with great caution that I pen my own experiences and my own observations along this line. Some of them I witnessed personally and can vouch for with my own eyes. Others came to me directly, in a manner which I cannot doubt in the slightest particular. I have eliminated from the following incidents any and all reports which might savour in the least of rumour or exaggeration.

At Bethune there was an *estaminet*, kept by an old French woman and her two daughters. She had assisting her a young French girl of about eighteen years, who had one arm missing from the elbow down. This girl was strangely taciturn, and our boys dubbed her "The Silent Partner," in derision of her shyness and quiet.

I had come to realize, however, that many of these French peasants who talk little, know much, and I made it my business to get better acquainted with this girl. Gradually, piece by piece and little by little, I won her story from her.

She, too, had been at Lille during the German occupation. Her younger brother, her father, and her mother had lived with her in one of the middle-class sections of the town. Her father, it seems, had hurried home from his shop upon the German occupation, and had found the Germans attempting to break into his home. He argued with them and then, with bare hands, attempted to drive them off. He had hardly lifted his arm against them before he was overpowered, and the entire family—mother, brother, and father—were taken out and shot in cold blood upon their own doorstep.

The girl was brought before the commanding officer, who passed her on to the officers' mess. Here, in a drunken orgy, they maltreated her until she swooned away. As she regained consciousness, she tried weakly to raise herself, and in so doing grasped hold of the door-knob. One of the drunken wolves, who had been a leader in the deviltry, picked up a chair and crashed it down upon her outstretched arm, splintering the bone in several places. Whether or not the subsequent amputation was necessary, I do not know. In any event, her arm was amputated, and until her escape from Lille she was forced to lead a harlot's life among the German troops.

This was the tale I coaxed from the lips of a reticent French girl who had been through a German occupation. She told it not willingly or with *braggadocio*, but as a story coming from the heart and one too awful to spread broadcast.

Another case comes to my mind, the case of one of our men who escaped from the Germans and returned to our lines. He had been shot through the hand. This, in itself, is an inconsiderable wound, and on showing it to the German surgeon he had expected nothing more than a casual bandage. The German, however, told him that an operation would be necessary, and they lifted him upon the operating table without further ado.

"You will give me an anaesthetic, of course, won't you?" said my friend.

"What!" replied the German surgeon. "An anaesthetic for a *schwine-hund?*" and forthwith the operation continued, while my friend was held down by a group of grinning Teuton soldiers.

What do you suppose that German surgeon did for a simple shot through the hand? In the first place he cut all the tendons of my friend's hand. Then he removed the bone from the middle finger in such a manner that the entire hand became absolutely useless and might as well have been entirely removed.

In one of the minor advances in which we engaged we returned without our sergeant. The following day, in a second attempt to retake the coveted ground, we came upon him. He had been captured, evidently while in a dazed condition from a shell-wound in the head. A rifle-bullet had grazed the front of his skull above the eyebrow, making nothing more than a flesh wound, but probably rendering him senseless or dazed for a considerable period.

What treatment do you think the Teutons gave this wounded soldier? I do not know. I only know that I, with my own eyes, found him transfixed through the chest with a bayonet, the point of which had been shoved into a barn-door. There he hung, mute testimony to the German treatment of wounded prisoners.

One of the boys coming down to us from a neighbouring sector told of an advance there in which they captured one of the small villages whose name now escapes me. He told me that as they entered the village—this was a surprise attack—they came upon twelve women, three of them wandering about crazed beyond all recall. Eight others were lying dead upon the public square, all naked as Mother Eve, victims of German brutality.

Another story comes to my mind which for sheer hideous inhumanity exceeds all imagination. One of our boys had been party to an attack upon a village some fifteen or twenty miles distant. There he came upon an old French woman living in a little hut to the rear of her former home, which had been burned to the ground when the Germans retired. She was the sole survivor of a family of five. Her soldier sons had been connected with the regiment which defended the village. As the Germans swept through, the French retired, leaving their dead and wounded behind them. She followed the Germans and came upon her boy lying beside the road, fatally wounded and dying.

By this time the French troops had been reinforced and were sweeping the Germans back through the town. The Germans came upon the mother and her son by the roadside. As they retreated, the Germans poured oil upon the houses and lit them, and one of these companies of incendiaries stumbled across the pitiful scene of the mother and her dying son.

It seems hardly possible that any man could not be touched by such a sight. The mother had a little flask of wine which she was administering to her son in the vain hope of reviving him, if only for a moment. But the Germans saw in this scene only another opportunity to demonstrate their lack of human sensibility, and over this wounded soldier they poured their oil. Then with a rough jest and an oath they touched the flaming torch to him.

I believe that the Rev. Newell Dwight Hillis speaks of this story, and I believe that he has photographs to demonstrate its absolute truth.

I might go on and continue to rehearse tale after tale, all awful, almost unbelievable, were you not intimately familiar with the beast who breeds these horrors. Perhaps you in America will *never* believe them, until they come back to you on the lips of your own sons, but there is gradually sifting over to you some graphic demonstrations of the truth of the tales which you hear.

Little Belgian children are being adopted now and then by philanthropic Americans, and it was two of these children whom I met one day upon the railroad platform at Schenectady, New York. Their odd, half-familiar dress attracted me to them, and I asked them, first in English and then in French, whither they were bound. They did not answer me, but a station attendant came up and said that they were Belgian children. I asked him why, if this was true, they did not speak French, and he informed me that the children's tongues had been cut out. Yet more. As they pulled their little arms from their muffs, they pulled only the stumps, for their hands had likewise been cut off.

It would do much to awaken you people in America to the real nature of the beast which knocks at your door if you could have moving-pictures brought to you of that sergeant of ours, hanging limp and lifeless, nailed to the barn-door with his own bayonet. It might make the word "atrocity" mean something to you if you could see the three crazed women of whom my friend told me, running up and down the village streets, hopeless maniacs for the rest of their lives. Perhaps you would be less gentle with your German propagandists, spies, and thugs, if you had seen those two little tongueless, handless, Belgian children on the platform at Schenectady, or if you had talked with the little servant-girl at Bethune whose arm was gone and whose life was blasted. Then, perhaps, you would be a little less ready to forgive the German people, and a little more ready to take up arms against not only their government, but those brutes and imbeciles who make that government, possible.

CHAPTER 9

Back to Blighty

I might go on telling of German atrocity after atrocity. I might sketch the picture of the old gray-headed blacksmith in a sector of our trench known as "Plug Street," who was found with his hands chained to his anvil, quite dead. His wrists had been pulverized, and a bayonet transfixed them like a skewer. On the end of the bayonet was stuck this terse statement, in a scrawling, German hand, "You will never shoe another horse."

I might tell you of retaking trenches by counter-attack, and of finding our wounded with their throats cut from ear to ear, disembowelled, or terribly lacerated.

Even in those early days there was ample and sufficient material for an entire book about German atrocities. As week after week goes by new chapters are written, and, when the last chapter on this war is finally penned, the subject of German atrocities will fill several large and gruesome volumes.

But you Americans are already hearing many of them, and a mere rehearsal of their terrible details would not bring them any closer to you. Even a graphic word-picture is not one-millionth as terrible as the original scene itself. It would be absolutely futile for me to attempt to describe the awful scenes which I myself have witnessed, or their duplicates which are common rumour in the trench.

Therefore I will turn to a rather humorous incident.

It was during the usual eleven o'clock "Hymn of Hate" that one of my comrades and myself were standing in the trench. For some reason or other I stepped away from him some fifteen or twenty feet, and I turned around to call to him just as a shell screamed overhead. It exploded about a foot above the parapet, and the fragments sprayed down into the trench.

At precisely this instant my friend felt the unmistakable nip of a "seam-squirrel" who was making merry about his waistband. Just as the scream of the shell signalled its approach, he bent over, and the rain of shrapnel-bullets sped by over his head. Had he been standing in his normal position, they would have caught him fairly and squarely. When at last he did straighten up, he had the "seam-squirrel" in his hand. For a moment he held it thus and surveyed the course of the shrapnel, as indicated by the new-horn holes in the opposite bank. Then he addressed himself to the bothersome rodent:

"Feller," said he, "you're the chap that saved my life, and I'm just going to put you back home and let you have a square meal," and back into the luxurious folds of his kilt he deposited the "seam-squirrel" who had innocently been his preserving angel.

On my last trip from our rest-billet in Bethune we started at high noon and directed our march toward Vermelles, where we arrived at six o'clock that evening.

All the way to Vermelles intense and unusual action of both infantry and artillery was noticeable. Heretofore Vermelles had been one of the more quiet sections of the line. It had been regarded as a vacation to be sent there. Recently, however, this same sector had become one of the most unpopular. Owing to its proximity to the trenches, increased fire was being focussed on it by the Germans.

At this time the French were preparing for a somewhat elaborate advance, and the preliminary trench-raids and minor attacks had a tendency to excite the entire German line in that vicinity and to direct German wrath at French and English indiscriminately. As a result, from a place of peace and quiet, Vermelles had become a scene of intense and constant action, and our troops, knowing this state of affairs, expressed themselves very pessimistically as we marched away toward Vermelles.

Here I again assumed my duties as a sniper, and immediately upon our arrival in the trench I took up the usual round of trench warfare as the sniper sees it.

Owing to the tenseness prevalent up and down the line at this point, the night was hardly less bright than the day. Star-shells were constantly shooting up, blinking, and going out. As I stood in a dugout on a little rise of ground I could see, away off to the right, the ebb and flow of battle as the French advanced upon the Germans or retreated before them, and I subconsciously wondered how much longer it would be before our lines would be illuminated by a flood of similar party-coloured lights that would indicate action, intense action.

On our left were the Goorkhas. I have already described the ungovernable tendencies of these chaps to revert to primeval man. Since my days in the front line I believe that most of them have been sent to the Egyptian front, where the nervous waiting of trench warfare does not wear upon them, and where their natural inclination for open, man-to-man fighting is given a better opportunity to display itself.

In trench warfare the Goorkhas are inclined to be extremely nervous and to fire upon the slightest provocation. The best disciplined troops never fire without a definite object in view, but the Indians have a way of letting fly at mere myths and shadows. As a result, close proximity to them is likely to be a warm sector of the trench, for they keep things humming, regardless of the necessity therefore.

Impelled by sheer nervousness, the Goorkhas on our left started up a stream of machine-gun-fire directed into the shadows of the night, and their excitement spread down the trench until our whole sector was in an uproar. Our own boys, however, since we heard no firing from our alarm-posts, held out against the nervousness of the position until almost midnight, when our front line listening-post succumbed to pressure and cut loose.

Immediately our entire line was on the firing-step, throwing everything we had in the direction of the German trench, which immediately replied in kind and with equal enthusiasm.

By three or four o'clock, however, it became apparent that we were all firing at a mirage, and the line quieted down, but not until a German raiding-party, taking advantage of the noise and excitement, had successfully put one of our machine-guns out of commission.

This was reported to us about six o'clock that morning, and five of us were detailed to go down near the machine-gun and do what sniping work we could in retaliation for the German escapade.

All day we spent in that sector of the line, taking pot-shots at a nest of Teuton snipers some four hundred yards away, who were neatly protected by a clump of charred and jagged stumps.

Of course I do not know whether we did them any harm. Our object was to keep the Germans "on edge" so far as possible; that is, to keep them nervous. Only incidentally was it our desire to do them harm in a physical way.

That night MacFarland asked for six volunteers to go out into no-man's-land to reconnoitre in preparation for a trench-raid on the following night. It was to be our duty to make a thorough investigation of the German outer defences, and to find out as much as we could concerning the strength of the opposing forces.

Of course we took with us only the usual tools for a trench-raid—our revolvers and trench-knives. Before going, MacFarland indicated to us that this was no ordinary raid on which we were bound, and after explaining what he had in mind he gave any or all of us a chance to back out.

But none of us withdrew, and so, toward midnight we set out from a sap-head that brought us within two hundred yards of the German barbed wire.

Across no-man's-land we snaked, dodging flares and doing our utmost to become an intimate part of the scenery. About twenty-five yards ahead of us loomed the German wire, when off to our right we saw twelve Germans advancing toward us. Flat upon our stomachs we went, and by gradual degrees worked ourselves into convenient shell-holes in the vicinity.

By the best of good fortune, and it was only good fortune, the Germans had not seen us, and they passed within three feet of my head.

After giving them ample time to put distance between us, we crawled up to the German barbed wire at a point which we judged would be in the vicinity of their advanced listening-post. Here we pulled out our wire-cutters and snipped a neat path through it to the sap-head at which our efforts were to be directed.

As we came in front of it two close-clipped, blond heads bobbed leisurely about back of the parapet, so we knew that our attack was as yet unannounced. At a predetermined signal we split up into parties of two. A pair of us went to the right of the parapet, two went to the left, and the officer and myself made for the sap-head itself.

Of course we had no desire to repeat the experience of our former raiding-party, when we had attracted the entire strength of the German machine-guns by the firing of a flare. This raid was to be as quiet and inconspicuous as we could possibly make it. Therefore, instead of taking our revolvers by the butt, we took them by the barrel and trusted to deliver a silent dispatch to any German who came our way.

At a signal from the officer we plunged forward and did away with the Germans in the sap-head, making absolutely no noise. One of them received the butt of my revolver on the top of his head before he even knew that we were within fifty yards, and the other was strangled by the officer without so much as a peep out of him.

Such luck seemed almost too good to be true, but we made the most of it, and the six of us dashed down the narrow sap-trench into an advanced firing-trench which, fortunately for us, was not properly a part of the German line at this point.

Into this firing-trench we went at full speed, and on coming around a corner of it I ran head-on into a German peacefully puffing away at his pipe. Again the butt of my revolver came down just above his ear, and he collapsed with little more than a grunt.

While I was finishing this little job to my personal satisfaction, making sure that this particular German would not return to haunt us, the rest of the fellows ran on and obtained a rather complete mental map of the surroundings. This finished, and our efforts still remaining undiscovered, we were emboldened to try for the lookouts in another sap-head.

Two abreast, we dashed out toward it. We were only half way to the sap-head, when word somehow reached the German line that there was trouble out front. We could hear them coming up through the communication-trenches, and at the same time the entire German line burst into a roar of machine-gun racket that made the night sound like the interior of a boiler-shop.

This was no time to try our skill on the Germans in the second listening-post. We hopped up over the parapet and endeavoured to dash across to our own listening-posts as fast as our legs could carry us. But our progress was slow. As each flare hissed up into the sky, we had to fall flat or roll into a convenient shell-hole. We had made scant progress in this way for the best part of a half hour, when MacFarland, who was with me, exclaimed, "My God, they've got me!" and grasped his arm in an ecstasy of pain.

I managed to get him behind a little rise of ground, where we discovered that his wound was hardly more than a flesh-wound in the arm, although extremely painful. I bound him up as best I could, and we settled ourselves in an unusually luxuriant shell-hole, hoping that the line would quiet down.

By this time the entire sector had become thoroughly aroused, and no-man's-land was alive with everything from rifle-bullets to larger stuff. As we were discussing the matter and the prospects for our getting out alive, another of our fellows rolled into our shell-hole with a nasty wound in his chest. Later a fourth made his way into the same cover. Those of us who were still able to navigate volunteered to help get the wounded back to our line, but both of them refused all assistance and declared that it was up to every man to fend for himself as best he could.

After waiting for fully an hour, the firing lulled a little. I stuck my head over the edge of the shell-hole to see how things looked. Not fifteen feet away I could see the outlines of the same working-party that had nearly found us on our journey up to the German trench earlier in the evening.

By this time a driving rain had set in and the definite outlines of the party were not distinctly visible. Our wounded officer, however, found the opportunity too good to miss, and, raising himself on his elbow, he fired at the nearest German, whose appearance seemed to indicate that he, too, might be an officer. Evidently he got him, because the German fell with a resounding flop and a tremendous curse. The rest of the party then seemed to disappear entirely, and we were just congratulating ourselves on bagging the officer when we found sudden cause to regret our impetuosity.

Evidently our officer's shot, flashing out from no-man's land, had attracted the German gunners. After a lull of a minute or two they focussed their fire in our direction. "Typewriter-fire" is what we call it—fifty or sixty shots in one shell-hole and then fifty or sixty more in another, and so on until all the shell-holes in that vicinity have been searched out. But fortunately they failed to locate our particular hiding-place, protected as it was by a meagre rise of ground, and toward morning we were able to sneak back to our listening- post, where we reported to our colonel.

Four of the boys had "got theirs" that night. None of the wounds were serious, however, though three of them were sufficient to send the victims to Blighty. The fourth had received a "cushey" wound in the fleshy part of his leg, and a few weeks in one of the neighbouring hospitals would bring him around O. K.

For the next two or three days nothing of any particular importance happened, and we went about our usual round of snipers' duties, but always with the feeling that something was coming. The entire sector was extremely nervous, and the constant action of the neighbouring French continued to keep us on our toes.

I remember how one morning—it was on a Wednesday—about two o'clock I was aroused by a particularly heavy bit of shelling, and I hastened from my quarters up to the front line to find out what the trouble might be. The shells were not directed at the front line, but at the batteries to the rear, and they seemed to be screaming overhead in a solid sheet.

As 2:30 drew near, we could hear them coming closer and closer. They seemed to have shifted, and were now sweeping the communication-trenches just to the rear of the front line.

At three o'clock came the usual "stand-to" order, and every one jumped on the firing step, thoroughly convinced that a German attack was scheduled for the immediate future. From three to four o'clock we paced nervously up and down the trench, awaiting the signal from our listening-post. At four o'clock we heard the rattle of musketry-fire out on our front, and immediately everyone was on the alert.

I hurriedly made my way to a little rise in the trench, while the rest of the snipers ran back to previously prepared positions about fifty yards to the rear, where they calculated on becoming a nasty menace to the Germans in our trench, should they succeed in getting into it.

From my chosen vantage-point I could indistinctly see about two hundred and fifty yards in each direction, and the horizon within this radius gave the appearance of being alive. In the semi-misty darkness of early morning I could sense the Germans coming, although I could not see them with any degree of exactness. But as the minutes passed, the horizon assumed a steadier position, and just under it I could see the Germans coming on at a slow trot, massed shoulder to shoulder as far as the eye could reach in either direction.

Our boys held their fire until the oncoming line was plainly visible, and then we cut loose. Meanwhile word had been telephoned to the artillery to give us all the help they could, but in those days artillery help, at the most, was usually about ten or fifteen shells, so that it fell to us to seek our salvation through our rifle-sights.

By this time the Germans were plainly visible, and individuals stood out and ceased to be merely a part and parcel of a moving, heaving line. On they came, until they were about thirty-five yards from our front line. By that time extra machine-guns had been brought up from the second-line trench, and we were letting them have the full benefit of two weeks of nervous waiting.

Twenty-five yards away from us, and the full effect of our fire became apparent. There were huge gaps in the German line, and the closer they came, the wider grew the gaps. Another ten yards, and the result was in the balance. The Germans halted. At this psychological moment, by some stroke of fortune, we seemed able to direct an extra stream of fire at them, and they fell back to their own trenches. But at least two-thirds of them were left behind, out in no-man's-land.

Following this, everything was quiet for fifteen or twenty minutes. But then, apparently in retaliation for their defeat, the Germans started a heavy shelling of our front line.

Ten of us were congregated in the trench at the mouth of two dugouts. One of these ran out under no-man's-land, while the other ran back toward the rear. I was standing at the mouth of the one that ran toward the rear and was discussing the attack with four or five of the fellows who were with me. We could hear the German shells sweeping up and down about two hundred yards to our right. Then, little by little, they crept up toward us. One in advance of all the others hit about fifty yards to our left; then another—this time in direct line with us—hit some seventy-five yards to the rear.

At this juncture my guardian angel came down and whispered in my ear, and for no reason whatever I stepped over to the entrance of the dugout just *opposite* to the one at which I had been standing. I had hardly reached its doorway when there came a scream like an express-train in a tunnel, next a terrific flash that blotted out everything, and then I felt myself engulfed as by a mighty blanket which weighed down upon me with tons of weight. There was no pain, in fact, there was no active sensation at all. Everything seemed simply blotted out.

When I came to, a sorry sight met my eye. The shell, almost grazing my head in its flight, had buried itself in the threshold of the dugout that I had just left. The force of the ensuing explosion had catapulted the earth under my feet into the air, and with this earth went myself and the dugout in front of which I stood. The entire terrain thereabouts had come down upon "yours truly," and the main beam of the dugout rested snugly in the small of my back. I was flat on my stomach, and my face was buried almost up to my eyes in mud.

But at that I wasn't nearly as badly off as some of the other boys. The four who had been standing in the dugout opposite me had been entirely wiped out of existence. Within three feet of my head Porky Pete's feet stuck out. The rest of him was buried under the debris which held me down.

Even as I took this in, I became aware of terrific pain. It felt as though a great knife had ripped from the sole of my foot up to the nape of my neck. At intervals this died away entirely, and I became convinced that my entire body had been shot away. I remember wondering vaguely if a man could live without his body, and then all worry about my body ceased as I found that I was totally incapable of moving my arms. Immediately I conjured up terrible pictures of how

I would look without my arms.

Until daylight I lay there helpless. The Germans continued a terrific shelling, and it would have been utterly impossible for any of my comrades to reach me. The entire trench had been destroyed. The parapet for several yards in either direction was gone, and anyone attempting to rescue me would have faced certain death.

At last, however, three of the fellows managed to dig a shallow trench, which partially covered them and enabled them to reach the collapsed dugout. Fortunately for me, I was in a direct line with their trench, and by seven o'clock they had me out; but the rest of the poor devils who had been with me when the shell hit were not taken out until noon, or later, of the same day. Of the ten in that laughing group before the two dugouts, only three of us remained alive.

I was hurried from the dugout to a dressing-station slightly to the rear, where the medical officer told me that he thought I was good for Blighty. I had no notion of what was the matter with me. I was dazed from shell-shock, and persisted in believing that my entire body had been shot away and that only my head was being carried about. At intervals I found considerable amusement in observing myself in this sad predicament.

During a lucid interval I saw a chap next to me whose condition was infinitely worse than mine and whose fortunes were no better. He had come over in one of the late drafts and had been in a front-line trench but two hours when a shrapnel, exploding near him, gave him a jagged wound and sent him back for a period of weeks. On his return he had been in the trench but a scant half-hour when another shrapnel picked him up, and this time he was pretty badly done up.

With this fellow and three others who had "got theirs" during the attack or the bombardment, I was carried back through the communication-trench to a little Ford ambulance that chattered by the roadside. I happened to be placed on the bottom layer of stretchers. Just above me was a chap with his entire shoulder and head swathed in bandages. He must have been badly wounded, for the blood kept dripping down and hitting my stretcher just alongside my ear. Try as I would, I couldn't move my head, and all the way to Bethune I heard this poor chap call for water and felt the constant *tap-tap-tap* of his blood beside me.

In Bethune I was put to bed in a convent, awaiting further diagnosis by the physician in charge. On my right was a pale, wide-eyed chap, who from time to time reached under his mattress to pull out a tiny, tin tobacco-box from which he took a pinch of something.

Believing it to be his duly prescribed medicine, I thought nothing of it. But as he continued his excursions under the mattress, I noticed that he endeavoured to take his little dose without being observed by the orderlies or doctor. Medicine requires no such furtiveness. Immediately my suspicions were aroused.

When the medical officer came up to him, he said:

"Well, young fellow, what seems to be the trouble with you!"

"I don't know, sir," replied the pale, wide-eyed individual, "but I think I have heart-failure."

Thereupon the medical officer felt his pulse, listened to his heart, and passed on.

The orderlies gossiped openly about the terrific pulse of this otherwise apparently normal young fellow. Somehow I couldn't help connecting his tin tobacco-box with his pulse, although I had no reason for doing so.

Toward evening the M. O. in charge came in and made directly for this same young chap. But this time, instead of asking him what ailed him or how he felt, he lifted the mattress and pulled out the little tin box which had awakened my suspicions. Then, with a muttered oath and a disgusted look on his face, he turned to the orderly and said:

"Another one of those cordite-eaters! Send him along and give him two or three weeks of rest. Then back to the front for him!"

Cordite is little more than gun-cotton, or nitro-glycerine in solid form, and of course is easily obtainable near the front. It is likewise a very active heart-stimulant, and as such I believe it is often given prior to or following operations. This wide-eyed young wiseacre, knowing this fact, had partaken liberally of the substance, and as a result his heart pounded like a twelve-cylinder motor. Such symptoms, however, are becoming well known to medical officers, and as a result "heart failure" on the front line is becoming considerably less prevalent than in the early days of the war. Cordite-eaters are given scant encouragement, I may add.

After the incident of the cordite-eater another load of wounded was brought in, and a Goorkha was put down at my left. Hardly had he arrived when my nostrils quivered under the most hauntingly familiar, yet unfamiliar, odour. What was it? Where was it? I could answer neither question. As the minutes dragged along, it became unbearable. I turned my head and scrutinized the Indian. Certainly he was dirty enough to create a stench, but not such a stench as this. At last I could stand it no longer.

"What smells so?" I asked the Goorkha.

His teeth gleamed, and in reply he shot out a mixture of English and native jargon. About all I could understand was a word that sounded strangely like "souvenirs." For half an hour I pondered. Souvenirs? Odour? I could see no connection between the two.

In a fit of anger, I at length called the orderly. He agreed with me that no odour like that belonged in a hospital, and, like myself, he suspected the Indian. But in reply to his questions, only an excited medley of impossible English was forthcoming. At last, in sheer desperation, I said, "Look in his pack."

The orderly opened it, and recoiled in horror. The Goorkha sat up, reached over, and pulled out a string of six or eight human ears, purloined from dead Germans.

"Souvenirs," he cackled delightedly. "Souvenirs!"

I presume that his family back home would require some physical proof of his prowess, and he, poor savage, inspired perhaps by his peep into the ways of enlightened *kultur*, thought that his string of awful "souvenirs" would be his best and most modern answer to them.

That evening the physician in charge, a major, and a captain came in to diagnose my case and to settle my future disposition. They looked me over, but as yet I was unable to find out from them what ailed me. I heard them discussing my troubles, however, and gathered that they would not operate here, but that I would be passed on to Blighty.

Immediately thereafter I was tagged and loaded into an ambulance which took me to Lillers, where we were pushed into a hospital-train bound for Boulogne.

All this time I had been in a semi-dazed condition from shell-shock. It was only at intervals that I seemed to regain my full and normal faculties, but the hospital-train brought me to complete consciousness with a delightful shock.

If there is anything wonderful in the world, it is a hospital-train. Here, for the first time since I had come to France, I rested snugly between *sheets*. And the *springs!* They were real springs that rode you comfortably, without jolting, as the train bumped over frogs and crossings. Then there were nurses, every one of them a beautiful angel. The doctors, even though gruff and hurried, seemed like no ordinary mortals. It was the first time that I had not had to shift for myself, and I thoroughly enjoyed the luxury of being wounded.

The food was wonderful, too. I don't remember what we ate or how it was served, but I shall never taste food as good as I did upon that hospital-train. It all seemed like a dream at the time, and I remember wondering vaguely when I would awaken and find myself again in the front line.

One of the nurses told me that we were bound for the train-head of a sector some distance outside of Ypres. As we approached the town I could distinctly hear the heavy shelling which has damned Ypres since early in the war. Here we were switched about, and finally, after only a little delay, we were off for Boulogne.

At Boulogne hosts of ambulances met us, and as mine was adjudged a serious case, I was despatched to the hospital at Wimereux. This hospital, however, was full to overflowing, and we new arrivals were placed in tents. These were huge affairs, almost as large as your circus-tents. Here heaven itself reached down to us again. It was early evening, and we went through the luxury of a real bath, with warm water and soap. Immediately following the bath, I drowsed off. My cot happened to be near the door, and as the orderlies and nurses went back and forth constantly, I found it hard to sink into real, solid slumber.

At last, through the exercise of will power, I did drop off completely, and immediately I was in the front line wrestling with a husky German. Through the darkness came a woman's voice. It was urging me to stop, and I felt strong hands upon my shoulder. I hung on to the German for dear life, and endeavoured to plant my teeth in his leg. But still that woman's voice kept coming out of the dark at me. It bothered me. It didn't belong; it was incongruous; and I awakened to find myself on the floor, with both arms wrapped around the leg of an orderly and my teeth buried in the flap of his trousers. Even in my sleep I still fought Germans, and I believe that my jaws would have been locked in that orderly's trousers to this day, had not the strange voice of a nurse awakened me.

My nurse was a veteran of the Boer War, and when I told her that I was a member of the London Scottish, she took an extra interest in me and told me that she would see if she couldn't get me home to Blighty. The following morning they held a consultation over me, and I discovered for the first time that there was a kink or a jolt or something the matter with my spinal cord, which affected my right leg. It was considerable of a comfort to know that I had something definitely the matter with me.

After the conference an orderly brought all my stuff to the side of

ONE OF OUR GUARDIAN ANGELS

my cot and broke the news to me that I was bound for Blighty. I was loaded into an ambulance and moved to the wharf, where a white hospital-ship was being rapidly loaded with hundreds of similar inert shapes on stretchers.

Still it all seemed like a dream to me. The transfer from the tense excitement of fighting to the intense, almost oppressive quiet of a hospital-ship seemed absolutely unreal. I actually kept pinching myself in an endeavour to prove it all, and all at once, either a dream or a reality.

The bed with a mattress and springs, dozens of nurses, the smell of the water, and the inevitable noises of a dock helped to bring me around to a full realization that at last I was bound for Blighty and for home.

I had just inhaled a breath of true exaltation when the grim spectre, Worry, again reached out after me. Suppose the Huns should pick this hospital-ship as a target for one of their torpedoes! I dreaded to think of starting at all, and seriously contemplated a request to be returned to some hospital in France. While I was considering the advisability of so doing, the screw began to churn and I resigned myself to my fate. My mind was fully made up that mine was to be a watery grave. Almost in tears, I confided to the nurse that I could not swim. She laughingly assured me that there would be no occasion for such an accomplishment.

That night I counted each revolution of the screw. Every time that it hesitated or spun out of the water in one of the huge channel-seas I was thoroughly convinced that we were taking our last plunge for Davy Jones' locker. Not a dram of sleep passed my eyes, and I refused to believe myself safe until I heard the nurse say that Southampton was only ten minutes away.

Here we were again loaded on stretchers, and as I came down the gang-plank, feet first, I saw the most beautiful sight that ever greeted the eyes of man. It was home! It was the Southampton that I knew in real life! Those spires were no mirage; those taxicabs were real; the horses were not drawing artillery caissons.

Stretched out before me in long rows were ambulances by the hundreds, apparently, and what looked like thousands of stretcher-bearers marched in endless trains to and from the ship. In the background were six or eight hospital-trains and, earnestly desiring to be put in a hospital as near home as possible, I called to one of the officers, who was in charge of the loading of the trains. I told him a sad tale of woe, but he neatly and curtly informed me that I ought to be thankful to be home at all, and that I should not be so forward as to attempt to pick my own hospital.

But perhaps his bark was worse than his bite, for I was loaded on a train bound for the hospital that I most desired, the one at Cardiff.

Three hours later we were unloaded from the train under the eyes of half the town. Cheer after cheer was given, and we were packed into ambulances which rolled with wonderful smoothness to the immense hospital.

Here my uniform was removed, and in its place I received the usual blue hospital-uniform and a "nighty." I hated to see my Scottish kilts leave me, and, although it was strictly contrary to orders, my nurse was kind enough to rescue them and preserve them for me until my release.

Soon after our arrival Major Brooks, who was one of the foremost surgeons in England, came in, looked me over, and told me that he would operate on the following Wednesday. I asked the nurse to wire my mother. She arrived on Monday.

As I saw her coming through the door, I knew for a surety that I was really at home. Then I knew that it was all over, at least for the time. My mother was extremely brave. I do not know whether she knew the seriousness of my injury, but she gave no outward signs of worry. With both arms clasped around me, she kissed me repeatedly, and I, baby that I was, broke down and cried like a three-year-old, while she did her utmost to comfort me.

Next to my bed stood that of a poor chap named Gilroy. My mother immediately made friends with Mrs. Gilroy. The mothers or wives of all the seriously wounded are permitted to spend the entire day with them. All of Cardiff's homes have become boarding-houses for the duration of the war, and the hospital kept a complete list of these boarding-houses and constantly referred the relatives of patients to them.

These houses, although they are not in any way under government control, make no attempt whatever to profit from the misfortunes of their boarders. Their prices are moderate, and all the comforts of home-life are extended to the men and women who stay therein.

In comparison with Gilroy, I was the luckiest of men. Poor fellow, he had it right. A shrapnel bullet had penetrated just below his eye, to come out at the back of his neck, and he was one of the seven wonders of the hospital world at that time. But he seemed to be in the best of spirits, although constantly living under the great shadow. When I arrived he had already been operated upon five times, and both his nostrils and his throat were plugged. He fed and breathed through silver tubes, and to laugh was tempting death.

Although our ward was devoted to the seriously wounded cases, there was considerable merriment, and as we grew accustomed to the luxury of illness, we fell back upon our old habit of grousing. The orderlies were a fruitful field for our criticism. They were never there when most wanted. They were usually out in the courtyard shooting craps.

I remember how one day, when one of the boys down the room had shouted a particularly laughable jest at a departing orderly, a jest that seemed to tickle Gilroy immensely, he laughed as best a man can laugh who has a silver tube for a throat. Then he stopped suddenly and became white as a sheet.

"It 's coming on again," he mumbled, and all of us boys began calling at once for nurses and orderlies, for we knew that poor Gilroy was in the process of having a haemorrhage.

The nurses came running, and the red screens that stood for danger-signals were drawn around poor Gilroy's bed. Nurses and doctors hurried to and fro. None of us slept that night, despite orders to lie back and forget it all. It was not until morning that I myself dropped off. When I awoke, my first question was for Gilroy.

"Oh, he's all right," the nurse told me. "They expected to take him to the morgue last night, but they didn't have to."

Poor Gilroy seemed to have as many lives as the proverbial cat. I last heard from him about a year ago. He had survived nine operations and had lived two years, despite all the Germans had done to wipe him out.

Wednesday, the day set for my operation, came around swiftly enough. I was all dressed up like an Egyptian mummy and carried down to a big white room that was directly underneath our ward. The smell of ether was no stranger to me. Indeed, it floated up from the operating-room into our windows and constantly made us drowsy.

The operating-room might have been a factory in full blast, so swiftly were they rolling men in and out. One chap came out singing, "It's a Hot Time in the Old Town Tonight." He had lost a leg about three minutes before. Another one kept shouting something about "the damned Germans," and all the way down the corridor we could hear him cursing the Germans and everything Teutonic.

Amid such encouraging scenes I was wheeled in, transferred to the operating table, and strapped down. Then some sunlight, filtering through a window, struck a neat case of knives. The orderlies were polishing and sterilizing them. They glistened like no knives that I have ever seen before or since. I didn't have much time to contemplate them, however, for a chap with nothing but eyes clapped the ether-cone over my head and told me to do the impossible—breathe naturally.

I took three or four breaths, choked, took another and a deeper breath, and once again I was at the front, fighting the Germans in a hand-to hand conflict in no-man's-land.

That night about ten o'clock I regained consciousness. I would have borne up bravely under the pain, had not the nurse, in a moment of forgetfulness, told me that I could have a nice chicken dinner the next day. After an anaesthetic, even a chicken dinner is not alluring. The mere thought of food proved the straw to break my stomach's back, and for the next two or three hours I went through all the throes of hospital nausea.

I shall not attempt to describe the pain and nervous exhaustion that followed my operation. *My* operation would be of *no* interest to you, and *your* operation would be of no interest to *me*, although I am thoroughly convinced that my operation and everything that followed it was the most interesting operation in the world.

I found, on discussing operations with other chaps in the hospital, that no one agreed as to the most dangerous variety or the most aggravating or most painful. One chap had had three toes removed on account of "trench-foot," and he was loud in his protestations that the removal of three toes was a terrific operation and unquestionably the most interesting amputation in the category of medical science. Poor Gilroy, who probably could speak with more knowledge than anyone else, merely smiled a wan, feeble smile and gurgled something like "Wait until you have gone through five of them, and then you can talk!"

For many long weeks I was forced to lie with my leg in a little coop, much like some petted pup. Occasionally they let me up on crutches, to wander about like a lost soul. Whenever I went out to get any air or sunshine, I was placed on a wheeled table.

One of the blessings of an English hospital is the weekly concert. I remember one of these particularly well, for Phyllis Dare, the soprano, was scheduled, and I happened to have known her very well in London.

All of the chaps who were able to stand it, were wheeled out on the lawn, and I rested alongside of a poor fellow whose arms and legs were both gone. We were in the front row. He was to give her a bouquet, as a token of the hospitals appreciation of her entertainment.

A sadder sight I have never seen. Miss Dare finished her part of the program and walked over to the chap who was to present her with the flowers. She took them off his chest, bent down and kissed him, smiled, and then, womanlike, burst into a flood of tears, running away behind a clump of bushes to hide her confusion.

But, on the whole, such concerts did much to cheer the fellows and to make the endless weeks of routine in the hospital a little more bearable.

That night, however, the cheering effect of the concert was blasted by the departure of old "Shaggy" Grimes. "Shaggy" was a street-urchin in his early days, and to the end he remained one of the wittiest soldiers I have ever known. He seemed possessed of an indomitable pluck. A shell had shattered his shoulder, and gangrene had set in. They had taken his arm off at the elbow first, and then at the shoulder. Finally they had given him up as hopeless. But "Shaggy" bore up under it with remarkable fortitude.

Day by day he grew weaker and weaker, until he was too far gone to go out and hear the concert of Miss Dare. When they wheeled us back into the ward, "Shaggy" was lying half-propped up on pillows and vaguely whistling an indeterminate tune to himself. In answer to our chaffing he replied not a word, but continued this endless, tuneless tune. Suddenly he stopped, braced himself in the bed, and called for a cigarette. It was immediately forthcoming. Somehow we suspected that " Shaggy" was on the last lap of his journey to the Great Beyond. He finished the cigarette, carefully brushed the ashes from his fingers, and then called out:

"Fellows, I'm going; and I'm going fast."

The next morning "Shaggy's" bed was empty. "Shaggy" had gone west.

"Visitors' Day" was another punctuation in the hospital sentence. Our ward was particularly fortunate on these days, because we had a number of "arm cases." "Arm cases" are chaps who have their legs and so can walk. It is their duty on "Visitors' Day" to straggle out into the corridor, look lonesome, and corral any and all possible visitors. The richer a ward is in "arm cases," the greater the number of "solicitors" it is likely to have in corridors, and the greater the number of visitors it is assured of having.

Our visitors were almost always complete strangers to us, although usually there were about fifty *per cent*, of them who came every "Visitors' Day," and so became familiar to us. There were poor people and rich people, and they all brought their little gifts and delicacies for their wounded soldiers.

Different ones would pick out certain soldiers and thereafter focus their attentions on them to the exclusion of all others. A little six-year-old girl picked me out and called me her "*beau.*" She used to bring me magazines and newspapers, and, although she could hardly spell a word, she endeavoured to "read" to me by the hour. At first it was excruciatingly funny, but it grew monotonous as the poor child spelled out word after word, so slowly that I entirely lost the context of a sentence before she half-finished it.

I have often had people ask me if the battle-front does not make God seem a nearer, more personal being. Be that as it may, I *do* know that Communion in a hospital is one of the most impressive sights I have ever witnessed. It is not uncommon to see either a priest or a minister giving Communion to the wounded. The little red screens would be drawn about the bed, and somehow it did not seem at all out of place. Chaps, who in their former life would rather lose a finger than admit that they ever went to church, saw nothing amiss in taking Communion in view of the entire ward.

I remember how one Sunday morning the Reverend Bailey came in, and how he held Communion for us, while my mother knelt by my bedside. I wept as only a wounded soldier can weep when he finds himself through it all, done and completely finished. Yes, the battle-front, though it be near hell itself, is mighty close to God.

I might continue on indefinitely with detailed descriptions of hospital life, of its sad and humorous sides, for it has many of both. But, at best, hospitals are good things to forget; hence I will pass on and over the monotonous weeks of convalescence, until I was transferred to light duties in London.

I had read of Zeppelin attacks in the London papers, but I hardly thought that my first visit to London after my return from the front would be signalized by Herr Zeppelin and his doughty cohorts.

I had just left the train at the depot and had taken the 'bus. It was about ten o'clock at night. Suddenly, as I was passing the War Office, the anti-aircraft gun on the roof crashed out into the night, and far up in the sky I could hear that familiar, thrice-repeated *plop* of distantly exploding shrapnel.

Simultaneously with the explosion, myriads of searchlights shot up into the night and wavered back and forth like long, lean, accusing fingers. Gradually they converged, and five of them at once focused on a great sausage-like object, which, under the blast of light, became illuminated until it shone like silver.

In a great curve the Zeppelin swung over London. I alighted from the 'bus at the Nelson Monument, the better to observe the raid. No one seemed particularly frightened. Perhaps we would have been if we had known how close we were to the danger-point. I had hardly been at the base of the monument for more than three minutes when there came a terrific explosion and a rush of air from about one hundred yards to my right. With the crash came a jet of blue flame that seemed to leap almost as high as the Zeppelin. They had dropped an incendiary bomb which had set off the gas-main, and only the ready action of the London fire-department saved the city from a nasty conflagration at this time.

After a shivering half-hour of expectation, the horrible failed to happen and the raid was reported to be over. As usual, little or no military damage had been done, and London settled back into the humdrum harness of its usual tasks.

After serving for some time in the lighter jobs about headquarters, I was finally given my discharge, as it soon became apparent that I could not stand either long marches or much standing, owing to a badly injured tendon in my foot and calf. And so, on January 21, 1916, I embarked for America.

CHAPTER 10

Who Will Win the War and How

I arrived in America some little time before your country entered the war.

During the past year or more, as an ex-soldier, I have been called upon to travel about considerably, and have had an opportunity to talk with many and to observe widely. With the battle-front ever fresh in my mind, I cannot help contrasting militant America with war-time London.

In the course of my travels I am asked the same old question a dozen times a day. It is always this:

"*When* will the war stop, and *how* will it stop!"

Here are really two questions which only a fool would pretend to answer. Anything that I may say will be only my personal opinion, and my only authority will be my experience on the firing-line and my close intimacy with America and her people.

There is not one iota of doubt in my mind as to *who* will win this war. There was no doubt in my mind as to the ultimate winner from the moment that the news flashed back to London of the wonderful stand taken by our London Scottish on Hallowe'en Night. Ultimately the Allies—and you are one of us—will win, and it will be no "Peace without Victory."

Immediately the pessimists—we need pessimists in order to keep our proper mental balance—will arise and sketch a picture something after this fashion:

Germany is today the winner. Territorially she has gained twice, yes, thrice as much as was originally called for by her ambitious program of militarism. Today Germany controls a vast and fertile territory which is far preferable to her and far more precious than her malaria-ridden colonies in Africa and elsewhere.

Yes, I will agree that today Germany is a winner in so far as territorial aggrandizement is concerned. But the war has only begun. It has only passed through the first two of its three phases. Back when I knew the smell of smoke and powder we were nearing the end of the first phase, the phase of retreat, of "strategical retreat" made famous and ludicrous by Hindenburg. During this period England and France were gathering their forces and were exercising their muscles in preparation for the struggle to come.

Then came the second phase, when these newfound muscles tightened and the line held, and Germany stopped advancing. We are now in the last stages of the second phase. We now know that those bands of men and steel which surround Germany can hold her indefinitely, *forever*, if necessary.

The third and final stage of the war is approaching, when the strength which we have been building up during these years will be expended in a mighty spring that will stop little short of Berlin itself.

This third stage may continue as long or longer than the first two stages combined, but it is near, and Germany knows it is near.

I have said that I knew the ultimate winner from the beginning. I knew it far better after I had fought the German and tested his spirit. What wins a war? It is the spirit of the fighter, reinforced by the spirit of the people back home and by the mechanical aids of your munition factories. *The German fighter is lacking in this spirit.*

Do not misunderstand me. The German is a splendid, a tremendous fighter, but only when he is fighting *en masse*. Individually, he is a coward at heart, and has none of the righteous anger behind him that inspires the Allied soldiers. He fights because he is ordered to fight, because he will face certain death if he does not fight. His arm is not steeled by the cry of humanity nor by the cries of murdered women and children.

It is because the German does not fight for the love of righteous fighting, but because he is ordered to fight, that I know we Allies will win. It is not in the book that the Germans shall come out victorious. It was not in the book when a mere handful of British stood off the German hosts at the Battle of Mons.

The ultimate victor in this war was forecast when the French forced back the German hordes at the Marne. When the Germans made their drive on Calais and failed, the victor of this struggle was again foretold. When the Belgian ports failed to fall into German hands through Ypres, the ultimate victor was once more prophesied.

Germany's early drive through Russia failed; at Verdun she failed; in Italy she failed. Always she falls short. And why?

Germany today, (as at time of first publication), fights as a machine, and machines have their limitations. Germany's soldiers fight as machines. There is none of the spirit in the German soldier to drive him on against tremendous odds. Had there been this spirit at the Marne, at the Mons, at Verdun, or at Calais, Germany would have been the victor today, and England, France, Italy, and America, too, would at this moment be outstretched in prayer before the feet of *Wilhelm der Grosse.*

Germany today is in a steel cage, and the bars are slowly closing round her, as did the walls of Poe's horrid chamber. Behind those walls, pushing them closer and closer, stand the upraised hands of all civilized humanity. These hands are steeled by necessity, for, should the Germans win by fluke or otherwise, the world from that day forward would become a tool, an abased tool, of German treachery and bribe.

The civilized world, whether or not it has formally enlisted on the side of the Allies, realizes this today. England must fight on, because, should she stop and should Germany become the ultimate victor, England's sea-power would be taken away. With it would go England. Commercially, she would be subjected to the point of extinction. France is steeled by dire necessity, for, should Germany win, there would be no more France.

And you Americans! Why will you fight on and on when your time comes, as we are now fighting! Because, should Germany win, you know as well as I where her greedy eyes would gaze. She does not want crowded England. She would be amply repaid, were England merely forced to pay tribute to her iron heel of the future. Germany wants a place in which she may expand, where her people may grow and grow, until by sheer force of numbers *der Deutschland* covers the earth. She cannot grow in England. There is none too much space in France or in any sunny spot in Europe. But no one knows better than you the colossal opportunities for growth and advancement in your own America.

South America, by evasion of the Monroe Doctrine, has already become thoroughly Germanized commercially and to a large extent educationally. Germany can absorb South America without South

America becoming cognizant of the fact. Until this war and the resultant hatred which it engendered, Germany could foresee in the near future the domination, the absorption of South America practically, if not politically.

The only spot remaining on this earth worth the seeking is your own land, and you may rest assured that, should Germany win the war, it will be at your fertile fields and teeming cities that the *Kaiser* will point his Judas 's finger.

Of course you know all this. I have merely been rehearsing an old, old story. But you do not realize it in its full truth and strength. Like the descriptions of a city in your geography of schooldays, it is nothing but black type. It lacks the life and truth which an actual visit to that city would bring. Someday, perhaps, when your first casualties come across to you in terrific numbers, when war reaches its hand into your home and your neighbour's home, perhaps then you will realize the full truth of what I have been saying and the possibilities that await you should Germany prove the ultimate victor. Only when you realize this will America be in the war as England is, as France is, as Italy is—in the war until our soldiers address their mail, "Somewhere in Germany."

Who will win the war?

Let me answer the question in this way. Place yourselves in the grandstand of a racecourse. Before you stretch two tracks, one smooth and straight, the other tortuous, filled with rubbish and debris, cross-hatched with ditches. On the smooth track runs a sleek horse, trained to the last minute, with a handicap of a quarter of a mile in its favour. That horse is Germany. On the other track runs a black horse, driven by an amateur. At the start the dark horse is a quarter of a mile behind its sleek antagonist, but gradually, despite the disadvantages, it decreases the distance between itself and its competitor until at the half-mile post the horses are neck and neck. Which is the better horse?

Germany, with forty years of preparation and training, after four years of war finds herself only neck and neck with her amateur antagonist who is running the race amid the pitfalls and perils of the struggle itself. Under these conditions which is the better horse, the one with forty years of training or the dark horse, driven by an amateur, who has equalled the record of its antagonist at only the half-mile post? Which is the better horse, and on which horse will you place your money?

It is because we Allies are beating Germany at her own game, despite untold difficulties in our path, that I unquestionably predict the ultimate victory of the Allied armies. This victory will come through no collapse of the German nation. Ultimate victory will be won, in all probability, by sheer force of arms.

Germany today is surrounded by her armies, concreted into trenches that stretch for miles and miles behind her front line. We will have to blast them back, sometimes inch by inch.

Today, so I am reliably informed, there is a gun—and by this I do not mean a rifle, but a machine-gun or one of larger calibre—every nine feet along the Allied front. Before this war can be won these mouths of steel must lock their wheels and stretch from Calais almost to Constantinople, a solid line of protest against the dream of Attila.

All this will take time. All this will take ammunition in abundance. To guide and direct the fire of this steel-tongued line will take the aid of hundreds, yes, *hundreds of thousands* of aeroplanes. To build them and to train the aviators will take time. To build up reserve stores of ammunition, fitted for days and weeks of solid shelling, will take time.

But in the meantime Germany is growing weaker. Father Time is on the side of the Allies. Meanwhile Germany is the losing winner. She cannot advance, and she faces an ultimate defeat as slow, but as certain, as death itself.

Her submarine, which she has held up to her believing and gullible populace, will shortly gasp out its last flickering breath of life. It may cling to existence tenaciously, it may linger on indefinitely, but its weight in the scales of victory will become ever more negligible. Germany's submarine hopes were built on a false conception. At first she thought that by torpedoing ships she would frighten the seamen from their duty. In this belief she erred. Then by sinking *sperlos versinkt*, or "without leaving any trace," she thought to reinforce the horror of her submarine and to inspire in all seafaring men such a terror of her "frightfulness" that they would refuse to man the ships. England would thus be starved, and America would be cut off from all participation in the war. In this belief she likewise erred, but not without extending "frightfulness" to its uttermost limits.

Can you Americans imagine anything more horrible than sinking a peaceful, neutral ship laden with inoffensive men and women! Germans can. They can sink such a ship, and then the submarine commander can climb out upon his little conning-tower and direct the life-boats to gather together and to link themselves with rope, so that he may the better "tow them nearer land." Then the German submarine commander can tie one end of this hawser to his damnable craft and submerge for fifty or one hundred feet, towing the entire company down to an icy depth below the billows of the North Sea.

But even this hell-born program failed, and today the submarine is gasping out its life. It is proving merely a tonic to recruiting in England and in your country. It is proving a boomerang to Germany. It has aroused the world against Germany as nothing else could, and it will ultimately go the way of the Zeppelin, a proven failure so far as military effectiveness is concerned.

There are those who would like to see the end of this war come quickly through a Germany starved into subjection. I, too, would like to hold out this hope, but I cannot. Germany today has under cultivation, with truly Teutonic efficiency, a tremendous acreage of land. This is being cultivated by her womenfolk, whom she has trained through generations of hard labour to withstand the rigors of agricultural work. Her transportation facilities, while somewhat weakened by the enormous strain of war, are still able to carry sufficient sustenance to keep her people breathing and working. Germany can, and probably will, fight on until her people realize the utter idiocy of it all.

But will they ever realize it? That brings to mind the eternal question, "Will Germany become a democracy?" I believe that she will, but not until this war is over. The force that will democratize Germany will be the flash of bayonets in Berlin, Allied bayonets. You need not look for an insurrection in Germany until that hour.

Today the German people are doped with a hypodermic of egotism. They have no more idea of their losses than has a native of the Fiji Isles. No black clothing or crape is permitted to be worn in Germany, for the wearing thereof would disclose the losses, and the Teuton War Office does not care to have the people know how heavily they are suffering.

Germany does not publish a list of her dead and wounded. If you have a relative or a friend in the German army, you must go to a "*bureau*" and inquire privately to ascertain his fate. The aborted brain which planned this war took good care to see that its cost should be hidden from the people. And not its cost in men alone, but in money, likewise, for the German system of financing this war is based on a clear scheme of robbing Peter to pay Paul, and then robbing Paul to pay Peter back again. Both robberies are accomplished with the utmost skill and despatch, so that the victim never realizes it and remains dreaming as pleasantly as the Chinese opium smoker.

You need look for no insurrection in Germany, because the German people do not know what is happening today. My sister was governess to the children of Count von Bülow. She was in Germany until six months after the declaration of war, and when she returned she was tremendously surprised to see that London was not a mass of ashes. She was also agreeably shocked to learn that the English fleet had not been wiped out, as she and the German people had been led to suppose.

Germans today believe that they are the unquestioned victors, and they cannot understand why the Allies persist so eternally. Can you blame them, when they think that London is gone, that the British fleet is vanquished, that England is subjected?

When my own kith and kin believed these things after only a few *months* in Germany, what must the true native-born German believe, who has fed upon this Teuton camouflage since babyhood?

Furthermore, there is no one within the German Empire to start an insurrection. Bare hands cannot push back bayonets, and as long as the Teuton army remains loyal through habit or terror, so long will Germany remain an autocracy.

Germany combats disloyalty in her army by shifting troops back and forth so rapidly from one front to another that no spirit of dissension has a chance to spring up and thrive. Any sporadic mutinies are but chance happenings, and I am frank to admit that they might occur in almost any army or navy, except one whose men fight not for a fetish of militarism, but for a great, good, and just cause.

But when the German army discovers that London is not a smouldering heap of ashes, that the English fleet is not covered with barnacles at the bottom of the North Sea, that the band of steel which now surrounds them has tightened until their own cities are at stake, they will at the same time awaken to the fact that they have been drugged and misguided by a self-seeking aristocracy. Then Germany, all Germany, will turn like wolves at bay, and democracy will replace autocracy, perhaps with the suddenness and enthusiasm that characterized the same change in Russia.

In the meantime, with all due respect to your President, I would like to take issue with his statement that we are fighting not the German people, but the German ruling class. Permit me to use a homely simile and to ask a homely question. If you were walking down a street and a dog ran out to bite you, and *did* bite you, would you vent your spleen solely on the owner of the dog, or would you turn your hatred on the dog itself?

The German people today, (as at time of first publication), are the dogs, and they are playing the part of the dog. It is the frightfulness of the *people* that kills us. It may have been conceived in the Wilhelm-strasse or among the pleasant forests of the *Kaiser's* own preserves, but, mark you, it is the German *people* who perpetrate the atrocities. It is the common, middle-class women of Germany who delight in hold-ing a cup of water to the parched lips of a wounded Ally soldier, only to dash it away and spit in his face in derision. It is the German *people* who cut our soldiers' throats from ear to ear and who give no mercy, though they beg for it so vehemently when cornered.

Our problem today may be to wipe out German autocracy, but the only way to do it is to march straight through solid columns of autocracy-drunk troops, the German *people*, sodden with years of training under German propaganda.

My experience in the trenches would indicate that we need worry little about Kaiser Wilhelm or his sons. They are safe, far to the rear. It is the *people* of Germany who gave me my wound, and it is the *people* whom we must first exterminate before junkerdom will fall.

Only because the Germans have proven themselves such willing victims of the propaganda of the Wilhelmstrasse can you blame them. Even here in America, in your own United States, you see the willing-ness of some Germans to lay aside all rules of war and love in their mad efforts to further the progress of autocracy. You hear a great deal about pro-Germans in your country today, (as at time of first publica-tion), and you worry much about them. Personally, I feel sorry for any man who may rightly be called a pro-German.

The pro-German today is a man without a country. In your land he is detested, and in Germany he is hated with a hatred that knows no bounds, for he failed to deliver your country, bound hand and foot, into the outstretched palms of the *Kaiser*. The pro-German failed to give Germany sufficient funds with which to carry on the war. Not only that, but there are other crimes laid against him. He failed to en-list in the German army, as he should have done, and he failed to send his sons to enlist. Then, last and most terrible of all, he failed to split your United States asunder. All this he should have done, had he been a true German. But he proved false to his trust, and, like Judas of old, he is hated for his falsity by every true German.

Therefore, the man who calls himself a pro-German is a fool. He is not wanted in any civilized land today. When this war is over there will be no land big enough to hold him. His own country will disown him, and every other country on the face of the globe will brand him with the mark of Cain. The pro-German of today had best get on the winning side, not only openly and in public, but in his own chamber as well. If for no other reason than a selfish one, he will find it wise to align himself with the forces of democracy.

I have said that we Allies will win the war. Let me carry that one step farther. Every building, no matter how huge, has its foundation and corner-stone, and the foundation and corner-stone of an Allied victory is not your man in the trench, your picturesque flag-bearer, nor your gilded general. It is the unromantic, toil-stained, oil-bespattered labouring man back home.

In Washington today, (as at time of first publication), they say that six and one half men are required to support each fighting man. This being the case, when you get your five million men over on the fighting-line, you will require some thirty-two and one half million men to support them. In other words, thirty-eight million men will be withdrawn from normal pursuits.

There are in your country, I believe, only forty-five million men between the ages of 18 and 45. With thirty-eight million of them devoting their energies to war-time industry, you will have but seven million to carry on the petty affairs of peaceful times. In short, some eighty *per cent*, of your labouring men will be directing their energies trenchward, and it will require all their energies throughout every moment of the day.

You have no idea,—you who have tasted of war so lightly,—of the tremendous demands of a modern "drive." Only a short time ago we Britishers, on a twenty-mile front during a four-day offensive, fired more than eleven million shells.

Compare today's struggle in its hugeness with your own great battles of the Civil War. Your General Sherman, during his famous march from Atlanta to the sea, carried as his total supply of ammunition only as many rounds for each field- piece as a modern French "seventy-five" would fire away in some *seven minutes.*

Perhaps you will glean from this some little inkling of the enormity of the front-line's appetite. And every one of these requirements come from the hands of the unromantic labouring man. *He is the one who holds the balance of victory today.*

The side, irrespective of right or wrong, which can longest keep her labouring men working at their mightiest, will be the side to win.

Germany today would be much farther back than she is, had there been a sufficient supply of shells at our command, and we will not blast her forces backward until our supply of shells and artillery is doubled, tripled, yes, *quadrupled.*

All this spells only one thing—labour. It is the labouring man who must decide today whether or not he pleases in the future to serve as the tool of German autocracy or as the free servant of a free democracy. It is the labouring man, and he alone, who will put us in Berlin. Our air fleets, our ship-building programme, our *everything*, hang upon his beck and nod. Will he prove true to this mighty trust? He can make his bed as he wills—today.

And here I must risk your displeasure by criticism. But before I do so let me say that I know you will find the solution of the problem that now besets you. We had the same problem in England and throughout the British Empire at the beginning of the war. But we solved it; Germany helped us with her "Zepps." Today you face the selfsame problem; today you are only "muddling through."

In England at this moment there is hardly a soul who is not keenly alive to the tremendous importance of labour. You already know that over a million women are working in our munition-factories, but do you know that these women are not "working women" in the ordinary sense of the word. They are women of the middle, yes, the higher classes. Some work eight hours a day; others leave their babies at kindergartens and work for three or four hours before returning to feed their children, and then return to work again. In the department-stores, in all walks of life, you find society-women working as waitresses, as clerks, and as stenographers. There is hardly a woman in Great Britain today, (as at time of first publication), who is *shameless* enough to say that she does not work for her living. I know of men high up in the commercial life of our land, men who before the war had unnumbered automobiles and whose houses are palatial mansions, who today take it as a matter of course that their wives and daughters should work either in their own offices or in the stores or shops of England.

In short, every soul in England today is alive to the tremendous necessity for conserving labour and for making the utmost of every hour of the day. Every energy in England is devoted toward only one thing—the winning of the war.

Those fur-clad women who go down at nine in the morning to serve as clerks in the department-stores of London do not do it for sweet charity's sake. They do not brag melodiously of the number of sweaters they have knitted or the number of socks they have presented to our soldiers. All that is taken for granted; it is only natural. They do not even brag of the fact that they work. It is only the natural and normal thing to do in England today.

Contrast this with your country. I am a little amused at times to hear your women—and your men, too—tell of their mighty deeds of valour. Can you blame me? I come from a land where every nerve is strained to its utmost to win the war. I come to a land where the uttermost bounds of patriotism seem to be the purchase of Liberty Bonds or the knitting of socks. Wait until you get into it, my good friends, and then you will know why I smile a little sadly to myself as I compare England of today with your own United States. It is an unfair comparison, perhaps, and, anyway, you are not to be blamed. You are at war only diplomatically and to a certain extent physically. You are not at war spiritually, and for this you are in no way at fault.

There are a number of reasons for your present state of coma. In the first place, you never really went to war. You just *drifted* warward. You just *oozed* into the war. You were told before you declared war that you were "drifting into a world aflame." But so slowly did you progress from peace to war that the process occasioned you no discomfort or mental torture *en route*.

Furthermore, the war is a long way off from you. Its horrors are as yet unreal. They are a thing apart from you, just as they were in England sit first. Some day war will become a stern reality to you. It will burst in on you, and then the purchase of a Liberty Bond or the knitting of a sweater will cease to be the apex of your patriotism.

There is still another reason why your people are not yet fully cognizant of this war. You lacked a psychological moment for its declaration. Every war which you have had to date has been declared when some incident has aroused your imagination and stung your fury. In 1898 you had your *Maine*, and behind your armies, surging southward, rose the battle-cry, "Remember the *Maine!*" In 1861 you had your Sumter and your Bull Run, and the mob was stung by the insult to their flag. Even your Revolutionary forefathers had their little "Tea-Party" down in Boston.

In short, if you will scan the horizon of democratic wars, you will usually find some incident which has set off the bombshell of popular wrath and goaded your nation into action.

But this war had no such psychological moment, no such bombshell to fire the public pulse. When the *Lusitania* sank was the one large and thriving psychological moment. But for perfectly legitimate reasons you postponed action at that time. Had you declared war then, I fully believe that one hundred million raving maniacs would have risen up, and only a little heat, applied at intervals, would have kept you fighting hot while your swords were being forged from plough-shares.

But you did not declare war then, and in the intervening time your righteous anger petered away and left you cold and calloused to the lesser shocks that ensued. Then, when you *did* declare war, you declared it long after the psychological moment for its declaration had passed. You had lost interest in the thing, and, as a result, to this day, (as at time of first publication), you are at war only mentally and diplomatically. You are not at war *spiritually*. You are not willing to give and give and keep on giving. Your emotions still need to be aroused, for the emotions of a people are not negligible assets; they are not valueless. NO!

What was it stood off the Teuton hordes at Mons, at the Marne, and at Verdun? Was it the scanty stream of shells and shrapnel? It was not. It was the *emotions* of the men in our trenches. It was the *emotions* of the men back home. It was the *emotions* of the women who gave the men.

What America needs today is what England needed during the first months of the war—something to fire the imagination, to arouse the popular fury. What America needs above all else is someone who will snatch a brand from the fire across the sea and pass it on to the hands and hearts and homes of the American nation. Such a man will do more good than he who builds a hundred ships or makes a hundred thousand shells, for he will make America fighting mad, from boot-black to banker, and resolved to do her utmost, utterly regardless of the price.

I criticize, though I realize full well that today there are those who look upon the critic as close kin to the pro-German. Your country has been besieged with critics. You have had so many of them that they have deafened your ears to *all* criticism, be it constructive or destructive. This is not the right condition. Your great republic was built upon the rock of public criticism, and the man who silences criticism today is strangling the very thing that gave your nation birth.

But no nation, least of all your own, in times such as these has room for the critic who brings no constructive suggestion with him.

I hope to extricate myself from this class, not alone for selfish reasons, but because I hope to bring just a wee message to America, a message culled from my knowledge of England and the Allied fighting-line.

Today I think you will agree with me when I repeat that few of you are at war in aught but a diplomatic and physical sense. You are not at war emotionally. In your saner moments you frankly admit it, and you are inclined to smile with me at your conceit. You have not as yet begun to pool your selfish interests for the common good. Your workmen, even those engaged directly in war-time industries, feel free to strike. Your silk-stockinged aristocracy—some of them—do not blush at profiteering. You let your irresponsible rabble tie up the production of timber for aeroplanes and ships. Negligence or inexperience ties up the production of war materials. There is no crime in that, perhaps. The crime rests on *you*, on you who calmly sit and knit and give from your surplus to liberty loans, on you who do nothing and then like to say that you are "suffering all the privations of war."

But you are not. You know you are not. The war has not stretched its ghastly finger into your homes. You are not *really* at war. What you need is some awful shock to arouse you from your justifiable lethargy. What you need is a bombshell dropped blazing into your land. What you need is a *salesman* to *sell* this war to you.

Wars have to be sold to a free and democratic country. Usually they are automatically sold on the declaration, as was your Spanish-American War, your Civil War, and your Revolution. But this war, let me repeat, owing to the circumstances surrounding its declaration, had no such bombshell connected with your declaration, and the result is that someone must go at the job of selling this war to the *hearts* of the American people in the same thorough manner in which you have gone at the job of selling the war to the *heads* of the American people.

America is not "sold" today. The educated minority are "sold" to a certain extent. But how about the man in the street, the labouring man, the vast bulk of your population, the man upon whom the fate of this war and the fate of America now hangs? Go out and talk with the man in the streets, and then form your opinion as to whether or not America is willing to give her all.

It will take an appeal to your *emotions* to consummate the sale of this war. Emotions are the factors which bring about every sale, be it for house-paint, automobiles, or wars. Wars are *fought* by men, machines, and money, but wars are *won* by the emotions which actuate those men, by the emotions which actuate those machines and that money.

My hope and prayer today is that America will not have to wait until the clouds of war hang low over her streets. I pray that she will not have to wait until her avenues stream with maimed and crippled men. Before that time comes I hope that some master salesman, some human engineer, will rise up and touch the spark that will set your emotional fires to burning. Before that time comes I hope that America will awaken to the very uttermost fibre of her soul, and will steel herself with the wrath of a nation aroused to a fighting pitch.

For when your boys go over the top they'll want to know that they have behind them not just the cold, insensate money of the American people; they'll want to know that they have behind them the *heart* and *soul* of the American people. They'll want to know that the American people are going, over the top with them, and that they are fighting mad and resolved to do their utmost, regardless of the cost.

We—all of us—want America to be an ally with strong, hot pulses, and not just the pulsing of shallow, shoddy sympathies, because when the history of this war is written we want America's finger to reach down into every line. We want your impress on the book of German fate.

If you are to be an ally, we want you to be an ally fired with the emotions which fire Great Britain, the emotions which fire poor, shattered France. We want you to be an ally at war not with your men, not with your money, not with your machines. NO! We want you to be an ally at war with your emotions, at war with your hearts, at war with your inmost and uttermost *souls!*

LEONAUR

ALSO FROM LEONAUR

AVAILABLE IN SOFTCOVER OR HARDCOVER WITH DUST JACKET

THE 9TH—THE KING'S (LIVERPOOL REGIMENT) IN THE GREAT WAR 1914 - 1918 *by Enos H. G. Roberts*—Mersey to mud—war and Liverpool men.

THE GAMBARDIER *by Mark Severn*—The experiences of a battery of Heavy artillery on the Western Front during the First World War.

FROM MESSINES TO THIRD YPRES *by Thomas Floyd*—A personal account of the First World War on the Western front by a 2/5th Lancashire Fusilier.

THE IRISH GUARDS IN THE GREAT WAR - VOLUME 1 *by Rudyard Kipling*—Edited and Compiled from Their Diaries and Papers—The First Battalion.

THE IRISH GUARDS IN THE GREAT WAR - VOLUME 1 *by Rudyard Kipling*—Edited and Compiled from Their Diaries and Papers—The Second Battalion.

ARMOURED CARS IN EDEN *by K. Roosevelt*—An American President's son serving in Rolls Royce armoured cars with the British in Mesopatamia & with the American Artillery in France during the First World War.

CHASSEUR OF 1914 *by Marcel Dupont*—Experiences of the twilight of the French Light Cavalry by a young officer during the early battles of the great war in Europe.

TROOP HORSE & TRENCH *by R.A. Lloyd*—The experiences of a British Lifeguardsman of the household cavalry fighting on the western front during the First World War 1914-18.

THE EAST AFRICAN MOUNTED RIFLES *by C.J. Wilson*—Experiences of the campaign in the East African bush during the First World War.

THE LONG PATROL *by George Berrie*—A Novel of Light Horsemen from Gallipoli to the Palestine campaign of the First World War.

THE FIGHTING CAMELIERS *by Frank Reid*—The exploits of the Imperial Camel Corps in the desert and Palestine campaigns of the First World War.

STEEL CHARIOTS IN THE DESERT *by S. C. Rolls*—The first world war experiences of a Rolls Royce armoured car driver with the Duke of Westminster in Libya and in Arabia with T.E. Lawrence.

WITH THE IMPERIAL CAMEL CORPS IN THE GREAT WAR *by Geoffrey Inchbald*—The story of a serving officer with the British 2nd battalion against the Senussi and during the Palestine campaign.

Lightning Source UK Ltd.
Milton Keynes UK
UKHW031149020919
349001UK00001B/34/P